THE SHIP OF SEVEN MURDERS

On 25 June 1828, the *Mary Russell* sailed into Cork harbour from the West Indies. Seven crew members lay in the main saloon, brutally and inexplicably murdered by the captain. Survivors revealed a tale of danger and delusion on the high seas . . . The story of the *Mary Russell* was forgotten until Kathy Bunney located the grave of a murdered crewman. Now the facts of the case have been reconstructed. How would today's psychiatrists and courts view Captain Stewart's behaviour? A bizarre tragedy, its true story and dramatic court case are unravelled in this gripping account.

ALANNAH HOPKIN
with
KATHY BUNNEY

◆

THE SHIP OF
SEVEN MURDERS

A TRUE STORY OF MADNESS AND MURDER

Complete and Unabridged

ULVERSCROFT
Leicester

First published in the Republic of Ireland in 2010 by
The Collins Press
Cork

First Large Print Edition
published 2011
by arrangement with
The Collins Press
Cork

364 • 152309

British Library CIP Data

Hopkin, Alannah, *1949 –*
The ship of seven murders.
1. *Mary Russell* (Brig) 2. Stewart, William *1775 – 1873*- -
Trials, litigation, etc. 3. Mass murder- -History- -
19th century. 4. Sailors- -Crimes against- -History- -
19th century. 5. Trials (Murder)- -Ireland- -History- -
19th century. 6. Large type books.
I. Title II. Bunney, Kathy
364.1'5234'09034–dc22

ISBN 978–1–4448–0932–9

Published by
F. A. Thorpe (Publishing)
Anstey, Leicestershire

Set by Words & Graphics Ltd.
Anstey, Leicestershire
Printed and bound in Great Britain by
T. J. International Ltd., Padstow, Cornwall

This book is printed on acid-free paper

364 · 152309.

In memory of all
who have lost their lives at sea.

Contents

Acknowledgements

My sincere thanks to all who have spoken to me on the subject of the *Mary Russell*. Tanja MacMahon and her daughter Enya for the company and help while researching and the fabulous drawings that were produced to illustrate my thesis. The entire staff of both the City and County Library Local History Departments for the interest and direction that they provided. At Coláiste Stiofáin Naofa sincere gratitude to Shane Lehane for encouragement and advice that was paramount in the thesis going forward. My family, parents, brothers, sons and partner. And last but not least for the wonderful gift of Alannah who has done an amazing job bringing this project to its conclusion.

Kathy Bunney

Thanks first of all to Kathy Bunney for handing over her thesis and all her research, and giving me a free hand with the project. Thank you to John Fitzgerald, Librarian, Boole Library, University College Cork, and to his staff, especially in the Law Library, Inter-Library Loans and Special Collections.

Thanks to Jonathan Armstrong, Librarian, King's Inns Library, Dublin, and to the staff at the Bradshaw Collection, Cambridge University Library, and to Eileen O'Connell of Kinsale Library. Thanks to Dr Brendan D. Kelly for his psychiatric expertise; to Denis Hopkin for legal pointers; to Rev. Canon David Williams for theological enlightenment; and Peter Murray of the Crawford Art Gallery. Thank you to Ron Holland of Ron Holland Design, to Neil Williams, biographer of Captain Hosken of the *Great Western*, for his invaluable knowledge of Royal Navy records, and to Daphne Pochin Mould, biographer of Captain Roberts of the *Sirius*. And a special thank you to Aidan.

Alannah Hopkin

We would both like to thank all at The Collins Press for making this book possible.

Prologue

In the late evening of 25 June 1828, the keepers of the light at Roche's Point saw two square-rigged ships on the horizon, sailing together towards the entrance of Cork Harbour. At nine in the evening there was still light in the sky, the sun slowly sinking towards a dusky pink horizon behind the new arrivals. A swift pilot cutter set out from Robert's Cove, expertly intercepting the boats. From the shore it looked like a routine homecoming, another of the hundreds of voyages each year to and from this busy harbour.

The keepers at the lighthouse identified one of the ships as the *Mary Russell*, ex-Cove, returning from a voyage to the West Indies. They were not familiar with her sailing companion, the *Mary Stubbs* of New Brunswick in British North America, but that was not surprising. The sheltered waters of Cork Harbour, and its strategic location on the southwest coast of Ireland, made it the landfall of choice for many ships that crossed the Atlantic or made the six-month-long journey from Australia. In Cork, then under

1

British jurisdiction, they could top up their water after the long sea crossing, replenish food supplies, and send news of their safe arrival to their owners in London, Liverpool or Bristol. Then they would await orders for their next destination to unload their cargo.

The two boats hove to when they were intercepted by the pilot, who jumped aboard with an agility honed by years of practice and climbed up the steep side of the *Mary Stubbs* as directed by the ship's captain. Captain Callendar explained that the *Mary Russell* was under the command of three of his sailors, and would follow them in.

As the pilot guided the two boats past the twin headlands, the sailors all felt the sudden ceasing of the ocean swell that marked their entrance into the calm waters of the wide harbour, *Statio Bene Fida Carinis* (A Good Safe Harbour for Ships), as the motto states. The two men and four boys who had set off from Cork aboard the *Mary Russell*, bowed their heads at the familiar calming of the waters, and made the sign of the cross, giving thanks to God for their safe homecoming. They looked with wonder and relief at the green wooded hills of the familiar shoreline, a sight they had never expected to see again. The pilot guided the boats past Spike Island and Haulbowline Island into the channel

2

beside the little town of Cove, where the *Mary Stubbs* dropped anchor; the *Mary Russell* hove to, and followed suit. Then the sailors tied on fenders and lashed the boats to each other, so that they lay rafted together, exactly as they had done six weeks ago in Barbados, their last port of call.

Leaving Barbados on 9 May, the *Mary Russell* had been a happy ship, heading home on a profitable voyage, her hold full of hides and prime Barbados sugar. Her captain, William Stewart, was an experienced mariner, known for his humanity and kindness, sailing with a small but able crew. This consisted of chief and second mate, a carpenter, three able-bodied seamen and three apprentice boys, travelling with four passengers: three men and an unaccompanied eleven-year-old boy in delicate health.

But instead of a high-spirited homecoming, they arrived in stunned silence. Their captain was not on board, and seven men lay brutally murdered in the main saloon. They had been tied up, hands and feet, then pinioned to the floor with more ropes, and violently killed by savage blows to the head. The floor was still sticky from the copious amounts of blood that had flowed from their bodies. It was four days since they had been killed, and the stench from the putrefying remains hung like

3

a pall above the ship. The pilot on the accompanying schooner heard the story of the carnage from the only survivors of the voyage, four boys and two severely wounded seamen, as he piloted the *Mary Stubbs* to her anchorage. Curiosity compelled him to board the *Mary Russell* alongside, to see the bloody corpses with his own eyes. A seasoned mariner who had witnessed shipwreck and murderous bar-room brawls, he was shocked to the core by the brutal massacre that he glimpsed through the broken skylight of the *Mary Russell's* main saloon. He made the sign of the cross, as was customary in the presence of the dead, and said a silent prayer. Meanwhile, the sickly slaughterhouse smell gently wafted shorewards in a light southerly breeze on that late summer evening.

The news spread quickly among the shebeens and whorehouses of the Holy Ground on Cove's seafront, travelling up its hilly slopes to the more salubrious streets inhabited by ship owners and sea captains, including Captain Stewart. Here his wife, Betsy, together with her four small children, had watched from the window every morning and evening for the past month, hoping that her husband would be home in time for the birth of their fifth child, due any day now. William Stewart was a loving husband,

4

devoted to his children, a respected member of the local community, regarded as a kindly sea captain, popular with ship owners and crewmen alike. By the time the *Mary Russell* reached Cove, Betsy and the children were fast asleep, and nobody dared to wake her with the news. Word spread like wildfire along the waterfront, then up and down the hills of the small town: Captain Stewart was not with his ship; he had jumped overboard near Cape Clear, after murdering seven of his people. The names were familiar to many who heard them: William Swanson, John Cramer, Francis Sullivan, John Keating, James Raynes, Timothy Connell and James Morley. Seven families received tragic news, more shocking than any dreadful fate they had ever imagined for their loved ones, far away at sea. The *Mary Russell* at once became known as 'the ship of seven murders', but nobody yet knew why seven men had been murdered.

★　★　★

The next morning, a bright, sunny day, Reverend William Scoresby and his brother-in-law Colonel Fitzgerald were being rowed across Cork Harbour from Corkbegg to Cove, where Fitzgerald, a magistrate, had an appointment. The Reverend William Scoresby, Fellow of the Royal Society and Chaplain of the Mariners' Church, Liverpool, had been married to Fitzgerald's sister, Elizabeth, in Aghada, near her home, by the Bishop of Cloyne on 20 May. He was on an extended visit to her family's waterside estate. Scoresby, originally from Whitby, was a distinguished seafarer and scientist, famed as an explorer of the Arctic regions, who had retired from the sea four years earlier, shortly after his first wife's death, to take Holy Orders. His new wife's childhood home, an extensive demesne on the inland side of Roche's Point, pleased him greatly. A naturally curious man, and a highly observant note-taker, interested in everything, especially things nautical and scientific, he was enjoying the wide sweep of water between Corkbegg and Cove, with its low-lying islands and the busy variety of waterborne craft, when a fellow passenger pointed out the ship of seven murders. This is Scoresby's account of that fateful day:

About twelve hours after the arrival of the vessel [the *Mary Russell*], in port being myself on a visit at Corkbegg, on the harbour of Cork, at the time, I happened to be crossing the water to Cove, when a gentleman in the boat, pointing to a brig at

6

anchor, remarked, that 'that, he believed, was the vessel of which the crew was reported to be murdered.' Such an intimation, of course, produced an intense and painful desire to ascertain the fact. After landing one of the party, a lady, at her destination near Cove, we returned with excited, anxious and incredulous feelings, towards the anchorage. The rippled water reflected the bright rays of an unclouded sun in playful sparklings, and there was nothing in outward nature accordant with a scene of blood; neither was there anything in the external appearance of the vessel calculated either to indicate mortal con- flict, or to justify the rumour which we had heard. One solitary man, like an Officer of Customs, was seen pacing in ordinary form and step the starboard side of the deck. We hailed, as we approached the gangway; and, too much excited to speak in measured words, abruptly asked 'Whether a murder had been committed there?' The answer of the person in charge was prompt and accordant, 'It is too true; and here they are, all lying dead!' On ascending the deck we were pointed aft to the cabin skylight, where a scene of carnage so appalling was exhibited, as to tender, by sympathy, association and memory combined, the

7

impression indelible. Whilst contemplating the dreadful spectacle two boys, who had been witnesses of all its circumstance, made their appearance, and freely communicated the leading particulars of the sanguinary transaction.

William Scoresby is one of the earliest eyewitnesses of the terrible 'scene of carnage', as he calls it. He was also the first to interview the survivors of this catastrophe, even before the official Coroner's inquest, which began later the same day. Fortunately for posterity, William Scoresby, a trained scientific observer, took detailed notes and wrote up his account of the tragedy of the *Mary Russell*, from which the words above are taken. It was published in 1830, and reprinted in his book *Memorials of the Sea* (1835).

The following reconstruction of the fateful voyage is based on facts recorded by William Scoresby in his initial interviews with the survivors, and in subsequent interviews with Captain Stewart, and on the sworn testimony of the survivors at the inquest and the murder trial, as it appeared in contemporary newspapers.

Part One

The Voyage

1

The Cove of Cork

The *Mary Russell* sailed from Cove in Cork Harbour on 7 February 1828, bound for Barbados with a cargo of mules. Her owners are listed in the *Lloyd's Register of British and Foreign Shipping* for 1827 as Harvey & Co., and Pirie & Co. Trading boats were often owned by a consortium of investors, most of whom would own a share in more than one boat, in order to spread the risk, and hopefully maximise their profits. Only one of her owner's names has been confirmed: James C. Hammond of The Cottage, Cove.

Mr and Mrs S. C. Hall (whom we shall meet again later) wrote an extensive account of a visit to Ireland in 1840, and open their book with a description of the geographic features of Cork Harbour, one of the world's finest:

The distant appearance of Cork Harbour from the seaward approach is gloomy, rocky and inhospitable. But as the entrance between the two bold headlands — scarcely

11

half a mile apart, and crowned by fortifications — opens upon the view, its character undergoes a complete change. The town of Cove, with the island of Spike which forms a sort of natural breakwater, and several smaller islands, give interest and variety to a noble expanse of sea that spreads out like a luxuriant lake to welcome the visitor.

The harbour is one of the most secure, capacious and beautiful in the kingdom and is said to be large enough to contain the whole navy of Great Britain. It is diversified by other islands beside that of Spike; one of which, Haulbowline, is the depot for naval stores.

Until the end of the eighteenth century, Cove was a small village built along the seafront at the bottom of a steep hill. The Cove of Cork, to give the place its full name, was twelve miles downriver from the city of Cork, built on the hilly, southward facing slopes of Great Island, above a beach and deep water anchorage. (Cove was renamed Queenstown following the visit of Queen Victoria in 1849, and reverted to its original name, in Irish transliteration, Cobh, in 1920). Its strategic importance became evident during the American War of Independence (1775-1781).

Troops and supplies needed by the British forces fighting in America could assemble in the large, safe harbour to await a favourable wind before setting out on their transatlantic crossing. The British forces were a ready market for Cork's massive output of salted beef and pork, salted fish, and kegs of prime Irish butter.

While merchants in Cork profited from provisioning the ships, Cove and the village of Passage West on the western shore of the River Lee, the nearest deep-water quay to Cork city, also grew and prospered. The importance of Cove and Passage West grew again during the British wars against France, which dragged on from the 1790s to 1815. Cove became an Admirals' station, and harbour fortifications were increased, while the Royal Navy built handsome headquarters on Haulbowline Island, faced with cut stone. From Cove's Spy Hill, which gave the best view of the deep-water anchorage, spectators could watch as huge British men-of-war, and smaller vessels assembled, waiting to depart in convoy. Signals were given by firing small cannon, and by the use of shrill whistles, as well as by flying particular combinations of flags. It was a busy stretch of water, and there was always some nautical activity to entertain spectators.

Cove was also a convenient assembly point for ships from other British ports, bound for the islands of the West Indies. In the early nineteenth century, merchant ships travelled in convoy, with an armed escort from the Royal Navy, to be better prepared against attacks by pirates and privateers — privately owned armed ships licensed by the warring governments to attack the enemy's shipping. In 1806 there were 600 merchant vessels at anchor in Cove harbour, and 400 left together in convoy on one day. When an enemy privateer was captured and brought into harbour as a prize, a festive atmosphere would prevail among the smartly dressed officers, and the exotic 'Jack Tars' as seasoned sailors were called, who promenaded along the seafront, known as 'the Beach'. Some sported long pigtails and gold earrings; the less fortunate stumped along on a wooden leg, and some had empty shirt sleeves where an arm had been amputated after battle.

From 1823 the prison ship, the *Surprise*, a tall old ship known as a hulk, no longer seaworthy, but used for accommodation, was anchored in the harbour off Cove where it became a familiar landmark. This floating prison, which could hold several hundred men, was used to relieve overcrowding in Cork's gaols, caused by the large number of convicts, male and female, awaiting transportation to Australia. The first convict transport to Australia left Cove in April 1791. Between 1823 and 1838 over 5,000 men spent time on the hulk, awaiting transportation. By 1828 passenger berths for 'respectable people' to 'the thriving and beautiful colonies' in Van Diemen's Land and New South Wales were being advertised regularly in the *Cork Constitution*. Emigration to America was growing steadily too, with transports leaving for Quebec, New Brunswick (then in British North America) and New York.

By 1828, Cove was a small town with a population of about 7,000 inhabitants, with numerous shipwrights, chandlers, rope makers, vintners, drapers and a thriving red light district on the seafront, the Beach, known as the Holy Ground. Cove offered sea bathing along its shoreline, and was beginning to promote itself as a popular resort to visitors from Cork city and further afield. The mildness of its south-facing aspect and the salty sea tang were believed to promote good health.

Fota Island and Great Island form the northern side of the channel in which the River Lee flows to the sea; opposite were the villages of Monkstown, Passage and Passage West in the parish of Marmullane. The parish was bounded on the west by the liberties of

Cork city, and on the south by Monkstown. Monkstown was then a village of about 700 inhabitants, built on the shore of the River Lee beneath a deep wooded glen, with panoramic views of the harbour. In 1828 Monkstown had a large number of newly built detached villas and cottages near the waterside, chiefly used as summer homes by wealthy Cork families.

Passage West, nearer to the city, had about 2,000 inhabitants at this time, having developed rapidly in the past fifty years, owing to its sheltered location at the inland extremity of the deep water harbour. Its main street ran parallel to the shore for almost a mile, and was intersected by smaller streets and lanes, many of them inhabited by workers, who lived in poor conditions in mud cabins surrounded by dirt. Work was plentiful, as vessels of over 100 tons were unloaded or partially unloaded at Passage West, before proceeding to the city's quays on the high tide, and the cargos were transferred to Cork city by barges or lighters. The first paddle steamer to be built in Ireland, the *City of Cork*, was built in Hennessy's Boatyard at Passage West and launched on 10 September 1815. The advent of regular steamer ferries greatly increased ease of communication for those living around the harbour. It was now possible, for example, to live in Passage or Monkstown and work in Glanmire, on the opposite bank of the Lee, or to commute on a daily basis by water into the city centre.

Shipbuilding and repair work were an important source of work for both skilled and labouring men in Passage West. There was also a forge, rigging and sail lofts, and extensive warehouse activity. High above the town, a cottage-like Catholic church stood in Kilmurray Graveyard, which looked out across the wide harbour.

In 1826 there were two Protestant schools and one Catholic charity school in Marmullane Parish. A contemporary survey reports 'The children are educated in reading, writing and arithmetic, and are then bound out to ship-carpenters, shoemakers, smiths, tailors, masons and the sea service, and are also employed in sea fishing'. This is the kind of education that the three boys on the *Mary Russell* would recently have finished, aged twelve, and the alternative prospects open to them.

Frequent passenger ferries ran between Passage West and Carrigaloe on the opposite shore, a five-minute crossing. Access to Cork city by road was much easier from Passage West than from Cove. The journey from Passage West to Cork took about an hour and a half by road. There were over a hundred horse-drawn passenger transports known as 'jingles' available for hire. Passage, like Cove, was a popular destination for sea bathing and recreation. By 1828, Irish merchants were experiencing the after-effects of the Act of Union (1801), as tariffs that had remained in place to protect Irish manufacturers were gradually removed. The linen industry, as well as marine-related industries, were adversely affected by an influx of cheap, British-manufactured goods. This new trade was facilitated by the introduction of inexpensive, reliable, cross-channel steamers between Ireland and England.

The St George Steam Packet Company was founded in 1821, and regular steamship passages between Cork and Bristol were introduced. While an old-fashioned 'sailing packet', a small schooner or sloop, could take anything from three to four days to three or four weeks, depending on wind and weather, to make the crossing, the steamships regularly crossed from Cork to Bristol in twenty-four hours. The company also introduced services from Cork to Dublin, Liverpool and London, which brought about a great improvement in regular communication between the two islands. In those pre-telegraph days, regular cross-channel services were a boon to the many English-based ship owners whose boats made their transatlantic landfall at Cove. Such ships might have been out of direct contact with their owners for anywhere between six months and two years, and the Cove landfall gave their owners a chance to decide where the ship should best proceed to unload her cargo. Cove, with its many seafarers, was also a good place to replace crew members lost through illness, injury or death.

By 1828 the wartime boom years had long gone, the local economy was in decline, and merchant shipping was greatly reduced. The number of sea captains and able-bodied seamen awaiting a berth on a sea voyage greatly exceeded the number of boats leaving Cove. So when Captain Stewart came to assemble a crew for his trip to the West Indies, he had an unusually good selection of men from whom to choose.

2

The Ship, Her Crew and Cargo

The *Mary Russell*'s captain, William Stewart, was a Protestant, born in Cove in 1775, the second child of a mariner from Cove, also called William Stewart, and his wife, Catherine, née Carey. Captain Stewart was an experienced sea captain, popular with ship owners for his reliability and honesty. At the time of his marriage in 1815 he was recorded as being a resident of Chatham in Kent. Chatham was a large naval base, which is probably where he learnt his trade in the Royal Navy. Captain Stewart does not appear in the 1828 Navy List, so he was not a commissioned officer. However, there was a surplus of officers at the end of the Napoleonic wars, when about 100,000 officers and seamen were unceremoniously 'dumped on the beach', the naval term for losing one's seafaring employment. Stewart may well have trained as a midshipman and passed his examination for lieutenant, then opted for the merchant marine rather than endure the long and uncertain wait for a commission in the Royal Navy. His age in 1828, fifty-three, was not unusual for a captain, but certainly put him among the senior members of his profession. Among the ships' crews he had a reputation for fairness and humane treatment, an important quality in an age when flogging with a special whip known as a cat-of-nine-tails was still a commonplace punishment.

Stewart was a slightly built man about 5 foot 8 inches tall, with reddish-sandy hair. On 31 January 1815, he married a Catholic, Elizabeth (Betsy) Turnbull of Carrigaloe, near Cove. James C. Hammond, a fellow Protestant and one of the owners of the *Mary Russell*, was one of two witnesses of this wedding, which took place at Clonmel Parish Church (Protestant) in Cove.

The Stewarts lived in a south-facing house looking out across Spike Island to Cove Harbour. Betsy liked to stand at the first-floor window and watch the ships passing by on their way in or out of the harbour. Having grown up in nearby Carrigaloe, she would have known many of the ship's captains, mates and owners. When her husband's ship was leaving or arriving, she would call the children and let them watch. When Stewart left on the voyage to Barbados in February 1828, he had four children under ten: Henry (born 1818), Francis (1821), Margaret Jane (1823) and Timothy (1826), with another baby due in July. Captain Stewart confidently expected to be back in Cove by mid-June, in good time for the birth.

His chief mate, William Smith, a Scotsman, was an experienced mate, who had sailed with Stewart before. Smith had a wife and family in Cove. The second mate was a Swede, William Swanson, both being typical of the cosmopolitan mix of mariners to be found in Cove. (Swanson is presumably an English version of Svenson, as there was no 'w' in the Swedish alphabet at the time). To this day, the names of long-established Cobh families betray their seafaring origins: Rasmussen, Verling, Stromso, Carlos, Patchkey, English and Cardy are no more exotic to a native of today's Cobh than more typical Cork names like Barry, Dwyer, Murphy, Cotter, Broderick, Keating, Sullivan, Scully and Connell. Stewart itself is an Ulster-Scots name, more commonly found in areas in the north of Ireland that were 'planted' by Scottish Protestants in seventeenth century, particularly Londonderry.

The rest of the men on board have local names: John Cramer, carpenter; seamen John Howes, Francis Sullivan and John Keating, and three apprentices: the senior apprentice

John Deaves (aged fifteen), Daniel Scully (thirteen) and Henry Richards (twelve). The ship's carpenter, John Cramer, travelled with his own tools, and would be prepared to meet any eventuality that might befall a wooden ship on a long sea crossing. Given that everything that made the ship sail involved wood, and that wood needs constant maintenance and repair, especially under the strain of a prolonged sea voyage, the carpenter was likely to be a busy man.

There were also two ostlers (stablemen or grooms) on board to look after the mules, Timothy Connell and James Morley. Timothy Connell had family in Passage West. James Morley, also spelt Murley, was an Irish-speaker, with poor English. He most likely originated from the Cork hinterland, where Irish was still the dominant language. Young Francis Sullivan was the son of a Mr Sullivan who worked at the Custom House in Cork city. Cramer, Howes and Keating were from the Cork area, most likely either Passage or Cove, but we have not been able to trace any record of Cramer, or Keating, all common names in the Cork area, nor of the more unusually named Howes, sometimes spelt Howse.

The senior apprentice, John Deaves, must have been to sea before to have gained his rank. The company that sold the *Mary Russell*'s cargo at auction were the long-established Quaker company, Deaves Brothers of Lapp's Island; John Deaves was probably from a branch of that family as it is an unusual name. Daniel Scully and Henry Richards (sometimes spelt Rickards) were on their first long voyage, on trial for an apprenticeship. They had the chance to learn the trade of able seaman, and perhaps eventually progress to mate. Meanwhile, they were on the very lowest rung, and owing to the smallness of the crew would double as cooks and cabin boys.

Like all boys growing up in a busy port, they would have used the waterfront as their playground, rowing a dinghy as naturally as other boys kicked a ball, learning their knots and knowing their way around a sailing ship from an early age. Potential officers joined the Royal Navy with the rank of midshipman at thirteen. Once a boy from the labouring class reached the age of twelve, he would be expected to start contributing to the family income; families with over twenty children were not unusual at the time, and the elder children would be expected to become economically independent as soon as possible.

In addition to his crew, Captain Stewart had one passenger on board, an eleven-year-old boy, Thomas Hammond, the son of his friend James C. Hammond, of The Cottage, Cove. He was a year older than Stewart's eldest son, Henry. There were close links between the Stewart family and the Hammonds: James C. Hammond had been a witness at William Stewart's wedding, and when the Hammond's child John was baptised on 20 February 1822, William Stewart was his godfather. Young Thomas, described as a delicate child, was travelling in the hope of benefiting from the warm climate of Barbados. The dry season in Barbados runs from January to June, and the *Mary Russell*'s voyage was timed to arrive in late March. The hot, dry weather in Barbados had long been believed to be of benefit to sufferers of tuberculosis. George Washington, future President of the United States of America, arrived on the shores of Barbados with his younger half-brother, Lawrence, on 2 November 1751, and stayed for four months, seeking relief for Lawrence's tuberculosis.

Thomas Hammond was the eldest of six children. Because two of Captain Stewart's children have a godparent by the name of Richards, there is a possibility that the third of the three apprentices, Henry Richards, was a friend of Thomas Hammond, and was on board partly to provide the delicate child with some company, as well as to gain the experience of a long sea voyage. Of the hundreds of young boys eager to be on board and start their working life with a voyage to the exotic West Indies, Captain Stewart must have had very good reasons for choosing Daniel Scully and Henry Richards. The same applies to his choice of mates, William Smith and William Swanson, his carpenter John Cramer and his team of seamen, John Howes, Francis Sullivan and John Keating.

Voyages to the West Indies were becoming rarer because the pattern of trade was changing, due to the outlawing of the slave trade and the increasing self-sufficiency of the plantation owners in Barbados. The West Indies were not a popular destination with sailors, being seen as unhealthy and feared contracting tropical fevers (which were often fatal) on the dockside. Captain Stewart himself had declined voyages in the early 1820s on the grounds that hot weather did not suit him: it 'made him apprehensive of his head'. But times had changed, work was scarce, and a berth on this three- to four-month voyage would be much sought-after. Stewart would have the pick of the best that Cove, Passage West and Cork had to offer, selected from the great throng of seamen seeking a job in those economically depressed times. John Howes was an obvious choice, a large, exceptionally strong man, of excellent character, a good type to have on board for a long transatlantic voyage, when anything could happen. Sullivan's father in the Custom House perhaps helped his son gain a place with the owner's favourite, Captain Stewart.

The *Mary Russell* was a small wooden brig of 132 tons, drawing 13 feet under load, single-decked with beams. She was eleven years old in 1828, relatively new for a sailing ship. That tonnage would make her about 80 feet in length, somewhat smaller than an average whaler of that era. Sailing ships in the 1820s were much smaller than they would become later in the century. The *Mary Russell* was built entirely of wood, with wooden masts and rope rigging. However, her bottom was sheathed in copper to protect the vessel from shipworm, and also to inhibit the growth of algae and crustaceans on the hull, which would slow down the vessel through the water.

She was snow-rigged (a form of square rigging), the conventional rigging for a small merchantman. As a brig she had two square-rigged masts, fore and main, and a trysail (sometimes called a snow) on the mainmast rigged fore and aft. The foremast had three sets of sails: topgallants, topsails and mainsails, also known as courses, while the mainmast had topgallants and topsails above its trysail. There were three jibs to for'ard, with the bowsprit to carry her jib sails adding another 12 feet to her length overall. She carried a clinker-built longboat about 18 feet in length, hanging from davits at her stern, for rowing ashore from her mooring, which could also serve as a lifeboat in an emergency. The longboat traditionally was an eminently seaworthy boat with fairly fine lines, to allow its use in steep waves, such as surf, or wind against tide.

The quarterdeck, a deck that ran from the rear of the mainmast to the stern of the boat, was the place from which the captain or one of his mates controlled the ship, similar to the 'bridge' on a modern ship. Towards the stern, on the starboard side of the quarterdeck, facing to the rear, a companionway (a box-like covering that stood proud of the deck) gave access to a ladder down to the main cabin. This was a relatively spacious area about 12 feet wide by 8 or 9 feet long, the main living area for the captain, his mates and any passengers. The clearance between the floor of the cabin and the beams of the upper deck was about 5 feet 10 inches, a comfortable enough height for the average male of the time. It was a pleasant room, with light pouring in through windows in the stern and from a small skylight overhead in the quarterdeck. On each side of the cabin was an open berth, and at the front of the cabin, near to the sides of the ship, were entrances to the master's and the mate's berths. Between the two, amidships, was an enclosed space about 6 foot square on the floor, usually used as a bread-room (a small area that could reliably be kept free of vermin such as rats, mice, weevils and cockroaches that were endemic on wooden ships).

The area for'ard of the mainmast on the same level as the quarterdeck was the forecastle (usually shortened to fo'c'sle, pronounced *foxle*), and was where the seamen congregated (hence, the expression 'sailing before the mast', which indicated sailing as an ordinary seaman, as opposed to an officer). On the *Mary Russell*, as on most small brigs of her era, the living quarters of the sailors were directly below the fo'c'sle, accessed by a ladder and companionway.

These were the final days of the classic pattern of merchant shipping out of Cork, before the introduction of steam changed everything. Ships came into Cork with miscellaneous cargos that were sold by auction, the auctions being advertised in local papers. Almost everything was packed in wooden barrels (anchovies, herring, almonds, tobacco, Barbados sugar) or wooden boxes (Muscatel raisins, lemons, China oranges, pekoe tea direct from China). Then the ships advertised their departure, for Lisbon or Malaga or wherever, and sought cargo and/or passengers for that port. On her outward voyage to Barbados the *Mary Russell*'s cargo is listed as mules. In Cove the animals would be able to walk on board across a gangplank from the deep-water quay. On arrival in Barbados, the animals would be sold by auction to the highest bidder, either individually or in small groups, as was the custom.

Much of the trade out of the port of Cork consisted of live animals, described as 'on the hoof', whether beef cattle, cows in calf, bullocks and heifers, horses or pigs. Traditionally the animals were carried on deck, tethered wherever a suitable place could be found between the rigging, though some might also travel in the hold. In previous years cattle had been exported to Barbados, but the plantation owners were now successfully breeding their own herds, hence the clever idea of taking out a cargo of mules.

A mule is a hybrid: the offspring of a male donkey and a mare. (The offspring of a she-ass and a stallion is often called a mule, but is technically a hinny.) Both mules and

30

hinnies are nearly always sterile, so a plentiful supply of mares is needed to breed mules, and a plentiful supply was available in Ireland, but not in Barbados. A mule handler knows that the mule's reputation for stubbornness is undeserved. Mules are more patient, sure-footed, and hardy than horses, and also live longer. They are less obstinate than donkeys. Exactly the qualities that made the mule a sought-after animal on Irish small-holdings — good pack animals, nimble-footed on mountainous terrain, hardy, intelligent and versatile — would also apply in the rocky terrain of inland Barbados. In addition, their skin is harder and less sensitive than that of horses, and they are better at resisting extremes of sun and rain. Because they are a hybrid, mules are said to be more intelligent than either their donkey or equine parent species. The only drawback to the mule is that it can kick in any direction, with each of its hooves, even sideways (known as a cow kick).

Timothy Connell and James Morley would spend the passage out tending to the mules: feeding and watering them, keeping the deck clear of excrement, and making sure that the mules and the sailors did not get in each other's way. In the course of a six-week passage, they would have to find some way of exercising the animals, probably rotating them from the deck to the hold. The cargo of mules would inevitably make a small boat feel even smaller, rendering it noisy and crowded on the passage out.

3

The Passage Out

Barbados is the most easterly Caribbean island, one of an archipelago known in those days as the West Indies. It is a small island of 430 sq. km, about 34 km long, by 14 km wide. Travelling due southwest, it is approximately 4,200 miles from Cork Harbour. It is 13 degrees north of the equator, and 59 degrees west of the Greenwich Meridian. In order to pick up the most favourable winds, in 1828 sailing boats would follow a triangular route to the West Indies, heading due south from Cork, passing the Canary Islands, and on to Barbados, returning via a more northerly route.

According to the Shipping Notices in the *Cork Constitution*, the establishment newspaper of record, the *Mary Russell* left Cork for Barbados on 8 February 1828. The wind was east-southeast, and there were no arrivals on that day. The *Mary Russell* was not the only ship heading for Barbados; three ships had the same destination, including the *Hibernia*, under Captain Raynes. A fourth was heading for St Vincent, another Caribbean island, and the *Ring Mahon Castle*, a regular trader on this route, was headed for Trinidad. Another ship in the list, the *Sir James Kempt*, had previously been skippered by Captain Stewart on a voyage to Quebec. Gone were the days of 400 ships sailing in convoy with an armed escort. These ships would sail in company down towards the coast of West Africa, for a sense of security, but once out of the harbour would soon lose sight of each other. The full list of the small fleet departing Cove in the direction of the West Indies that day is as follows (the list is ordered by ship's name, captain's name, destination, and cargo):

The Three Sisters, Pollock, Barbados, general cargo; *Dido*, Luscombe, Oporto, fish; *Julian*, Creighton, Africa, general cargo; *Eliza*, Dick, Para, ditto; *St Vincents*, Copeland, St Vincent, do; *Bellisle*, Lloyd, Savannah, slates; *Sir James Kempt*, Bridge, do. Ballast; *Bristol*, Tripp, Jamaica, general cargo; *Mary Russell*, Stewart, Barbados, mules; *Hibernia*, Raynes, ditto, general cargo; *Ring Mahon Castle*, Evans, Trinidad, ditto; Providence, Warburton, Sierra Leone, ballast; *Ark*, Sewell, Gibraltar, general cargo.

The list of people on board the *Mary Russell* on leaving Cove was:

- William Stewart, master of the brig
- William Swanson, chief-mate (Swedish)
- William Smith, second mate (Scottish)
- John Cramer, carpenter
- John Howes, seaman
- Francis Sullivan, seaman
- John Keating, seaman
- Timothy Connell, ostler, passenger
- James Morley, ostler, passenger
- John Deaves (15), senior apprentice
- Henry Richards (12), apprentice
- Daniel Scully (13), apprentice
- Thomas Hammond (11), a boy, passenger

The voyage began in cold, wintry weather. For the two youngest apprentices, Daniel Scully and Henry Richards, this was their first experience of a long passage, and of those initial few days while the ship 'shakes down', and the sailors get the measure of other, the mates and their captain.

As soon as the ship was at sea, and before the first night had passed, it was traditional for watches to be selected. There were two watches, larboard (port) or mate's, and starboard or second mate's. They worked four hours on, four hours off, with the watches between 4 p.m. and 8 p.m. divided into short two-hour shifts (known as dogwatches), neatly ensuring that the hours worked by each team varied on alternate days.

On the voyage out there were two mates, three seamen, and three boys. The carpenter, John Cramer, probably also stood watch. The captain and the ostlers in charge of the mules, Timothy Connell and James Morley, did not stand watches, but could be called on in emergencies. So there would be a mate, two seamen and a boy on each watch. It was a small crew by Royal Navy standards, but probably about average in the merchant navy.

One young man who went to sea 'before the mast', Richard Henry Dana, has left a detailed account of the daily routine on board an American merchant ship in 1832, which would not have been greatly different from that experienced by John Deaves, Daniel Scully and Henry Richards. Unlike Dana, who had been a student at Harvard before going to sea (in the hope that the change would relieve a chronic eye condition), Scully and Richards had a good idea what to expect, and had probably already sailed as foredeck hands with family friends and neighbours on shorter voyages.

Dana, who was to have a distinguished career as a specialist in maritime law, comments on the god-like position of the captain, lord of all he surveys: 'He stands no watch, comes and goes when he pleases, and is accountable to no one, and must be obeyed in everything.' This is the first and most important lesson anyone going to sea in those days had to learn: the captain's orders were to be obeyed unquestioningly, even when they seemed wrong or unreasonable. A ship at sea is not subject to the normal laws of the land: at sea there is only one judge, jury and enforcer of the rules — the captain. As the saying has it, 'the captain's word is law'. Dana's brig, *Pilgrim*, sailed on 14 August 1834 from Boston.

During Dana's first watch a storm blew up, and when he went below he fell victim to 'strong symptoms of seasickness'. Nevertheless, when, as he feared, all hands were called on deck to take in sail, he not only had to go on deck, but was sent aloft for the first time in the pitch dark to reef the topsails. He writes: 'I could not have been of much service, for I remember having been sick several times before I left the topsail yard.' The storm continued for the next three days. Having finished washing down the deck on the third day, an operation that regularly took two hours, Dana, who had not eaten for three days, was sitting on a spar waiting for his breakfast, when an officer spotted him in this idle post. He was ordered to 'slush' the mainmast, from the royal-masthead down, and knew there was no way out of it: 'So I took my bucket of grease and climbed up to the royal-masthead. Here the rocking of the vessel, which increases the higher you go from the foot of the mast, which is the fulcrum of the lever, and the smell of the grease, upset my stomach again, and I was not a little rejoiced when I got down to the comparative *terra firma* of the deck.'

When, finally, he is given his breakfast, he notes: 'I cannot describe the change which half a pound of cold salt beef and a biscuit or two produced in me . . . '

The going might have been rough for the first weeks after leaving Cork Harbour in February 1828, but Captain Stewart had a reputation for kindness, and it is unlikely that he treated his 'new boys', Daniel Scully and Henry Richards, to the cruel initiation endured by Richard Henry Dana.

Not all apprentices had such a tough time. William Scoresby, the same man who boarded the *Mary Russell* in Cork Harbour, and whose account of her journey is an important source for this one, first went to sea aged ten, having tricked his father, a whaling captain, into weighing anchor while he was still on board. He writes of his first voyage:

Not being subject to sea-sickness — the bane of most young adventurers — I experienced little of what I conceived to be hardship, and was in general not only contented with my situation, but lively, active and happy . . . All that I learnt in nautical affairs was something of steering, and the names and uses of all the ropes. I learnt the ropes in the following manner: I first enquired their uses and finding braces were for turning the yards, reef tackles were for drawing up the edges of the sails etc, I proceeded aloft, and observing the attachments of each rope to the sail or yard, I instantly knew its use and its name, then pulling on the lower part and tracing it to the deck, I noticed to what pin or cleat it was belayed. In this way, visiting many times each mast and yard and frequently conning over the names of the ropes about the deck, I soon became master of the subject.

Learning the ropes was an essential part of the apprentices' job. While there might have been some chain used in the lower connecting areas, all the rigging itself would be made of rope, that is to say, vegetable fibre, usually hemp. Each rope had its name: halyard, sheet, anchor warp, mooring rope, lead line. The latter was used to take soundings of the depth of water beneath the ship. The standing rigging, which holds the mast in place, would usually be 'paid', that is to say, heavy rope with thinner rope wrapped around it, bound together with tar. Good rope well looked after was essential for safety. Ropes had to be kept free of kinks at all times, and as most ropes are right-handed, it was always coiled clockwise. Before putting spare coils of rope away in the lazarette, a compartment in the floor of the main cabin designed for that purpose, first it had to be clean and dry. During a long voyage it would be brought on deck occasionally for sunning and airing. The apprentices would be expected to master seaman's knots, bends (joining the ends of two ropes) and hitches (securing a rope to another object), and also the art of splicing — joining ropes together — and whipping, the use of twine to prevent the ends of ropes becoming frayed. On a long passage like this one, there would be plenty of time to practise such skills. Traditionally, the older, more experienced seamen like John Howes, the oldest sailor on board, were generous and patient in passing on their knowledge.

Tar was also an essential part of life at sea, used for waterproofing and protection, and barrels of tar were always carried on board. The gaps between the planks of the ship were kept watertight by caulking, in which oakum (bits of old rope mixed with tar) was forced into the cracks with iron tools and then sealed with hot tar. Tar was also used to waterproof the seamen's hats and coats. Both boats and men would have had a strong whiff of the black stuff, hence the nickname for seamen of this era, Jack Tars.

* * *

The *Mary Russell*'s outward journey passed without major incident. Before leaving Cove, the chief mate William Swanson somehow caused offence to the captain. He was put out of the main cabin, and demoted to second mate. His place was taken by William Smith, the Scotsman. Smith was a veteran of the Royal Navy, and became a great favourite of the captain, sleeping in the berth next to his, and was frequently invited to take a glass of grog with him.

The crew agreed that Captain Stewart was a good captain with a pleasant disposition, who did not indulge in over-strict discipline like some of his contemporaries. In the words of John Howes, able seaman, 'He was a kind, good master of a ship'. When punishment was needed, he preferred tying to flogging. On most ships, the tying up of a man with his hands in front of him was a preliminary to flogging. In some ships, the man being punished was tied to a mast for a certain length of time, so that all the crew could witness his disgrace, and then he was released, in the hope that this had been enough punishment. There was only one incident aboard the *Mary Russell* on the outward journey: the senior apprentice John Deaves was beaten for cursing the ship. This sounds like the kind of beating delivered by a schoolmaster, rather than a serious flogging.

In the Royal Navy at this time, both men and boys were given a stiff daily ration of grog (strong spirits), usually rum. On the *Mary Russell* only the Captain had access to hard liquor. Captain Stewart was a devout Protestant, and his denial of the grog ration was, according to his beliefs, an expression of concern for the welfare of his men, all of whom were Catholics. Captain Stewart favoured temperance among his men, even though he made an exception for himself. The men would have known before embarking that the *Mary Russell* was a dry ship. They had other pleasures, chiefly tobacco, which they chewed, or smoked in clay pipes. Seaman John Howes was seldom without a clay pipe clamped between his teeth.

On the outward voyage the usual routines were observed, including the daily swabbing of the decks, more necessary than usual because of the cargo of mules. Another daily ritual was the mate's task of keeping the ship's log, and the charting of her current position when the sun was at its highest point. Captain Stewart needed to guide his brig across 4,200 miles of open sea to reach the relatively small speck that was the island of Barbados in the shortest possible time. Time was money, and sea captains prided themselves on being able to navigate accurately and get there and back as quickly as possible, to maximise their owners' profits.

While at sea, every day at noon, the direction of travel was ascertained from the ship's compass, and the speed was determined from a log reel thrown overboard, and timed against the sand-glass (a simple egg-timer-like device). The resulting position was plotted on a chart, and comments noted alongside.

Dead reckoning is a simple system, which just about anyone can master. There is an old seafaring saying that navigation by dead reckoning is easy because if it wasn't you couldn't teach it to sailors, a joke that reflects the low opinion of the intelligence of seamen. Maths may not have been a strong point, but sailors were intensely aware of their natural surroundings, and took a wide range of factors into account when planning their course. They used a vast store of sea lore, the accumulated wisdom of generations of sailors, which relied on close observation of the set of tide and current, the feel of the swell of the sea (which can be persistent and from the same direction), the colour of the water, the cloud formations and atmospheric conditions, the type of birds encountered and their flight, and even, in these pre-steam days, the smell of land as the ship came near to it.

Given clear skies, it is easy enough to calculate latitude, so the old sailing ships used to head for the latitude on which their destination lay, and sail along it, hoping they had made the correct decision when deciding whether to head west or east. To get an accurate longitude position is a more complicated matter, using a sextant to measure the angle between the horizon, and the sun, moon, or specific stars, and an accurate chronometer. This measurement was always taken by Captain Stewart himself. He was the only one on board who had the expertise to carry out the calculations and consult the printed tables (Nautical Ephemeris Tables) that would confirm the ship's longitude position.

Between Cove and Barbados, the *Mary Russell* would be alone in the vast empty spaces of the sea for day after day, and alone for night after night with the magnificent panorama of the night sky. On the rare occasions when she would speak with another vessel (the expression for a verbal exchange with another ship, which whalers called 'a gam'), the most important matter was to exchange the figures they each had for their position, their estimate of latitude and longitude.

The seaman John Howes showed a great interest in mastering celestial navigation, and enjoyed the challenge of 'pointing out the tables' to his captain. Captain Stewart was so pleased with his interest that on one occasion, following a successful observation, he invited Howes to take a glass of grog with him in the main cabin, a rare privilege for a plain seaman. Howes was keen to take more formal lessons in navigation, but because the ship was encumbered with the cargo of mules, Captain Stewart did not give him lessons on the outward journey, but promised to teach him on the passage home.

Howes was the oldest seaman (apart from

the captain) on board, a big man, and extremely strong. Most sailors were worn out by the age of forty, and retired to some shore-based occupation, so as the oldest man on board, Howes would probably have been in his forties. He had hoped to travel as mate or second mate on the *Mary Russell*'s Barbados voyage. We know that Captain Stewart chose William Smith because he had sailed with him before, but we do not know why he chose the Swede, William Swanson (and then demoted him), over the equally well-qualified local man, John Howes. Perhaps the offer of navigation lessons was an attempt to make up for what Captain Stewart perceived as a slight to Howes, and an expression of gratitude to him for having agreed to ship as a seaman, when a berth as mate was not on offer.

In the Royal Navy, only a hundred years earlier, the unauthorised keeping of navigation records by common sailors was a hanging offence. Too much knowledge among the common sailors was held to be a bad thing, and a potential source of mutiny: as long as only the captain knew the ship's position, his sailors were unlikely to rise up and kill him. The ban on sailors keeping navigation records was strictly enforced. Dava Sobel in *Longitude* cites the example of an unnamed seaman who kept a surreptitious record of the location of the fleet of five ships of the line during a cloudy and foggy passage home from Gibraltar. The navigators were summoned to decide their probable location, and all agreed that the fleet was safely west of the Ile d'Ouessant. On 21 October 1707, Admiral Sir Clowdisley Shovell was approached by a sailor for the crew of the *Association*, who had kept his own record all through the voyage, and disagreed with this reckoning. By his calculations the fleet was heading straight for the rocks near the Scilly Isles. He was hanged for mutiny on the spot. In the fog of the night of 22 October, the *Association* struck rocks off the Scillies, and sank within minutes, drowning all hands. Another three of the five warships sank soon after, drowning 2,000 of Sir Clowdisley's troops. This incident led to the Longitude Act of 1714. This established a Board of Longitude which offered a prize of £20,000 to anyone who could solve the longitude problem. The answer turned out to be an accurate shipboard chronometer, and the Board was disbanded in 1828, the year of the *Mary Russell*'s voyage. By then, all ships on long passages would have at least one chronometer on board.

As the *Mary Russell* sailed south and west,

the days grew longer and the weather warmer. It was the custom to take bearings off the islands of Tenerife or La Palma in the Canaries, to confirm that the ship was on course. By then the sailors would have changed into lightweight clothing, and be enjoying blue skies and sun.

4

A Prophetic Dream

The *Mary Russell* stayed longer than usual in
Barbados, but we do not know why.
Merchant ships of her size would usually
unload their cargo and reload with their
homebound goods in about ten days. Smith
mentions in his testimony in court that the
captain was angry with him for a delay about
shipping sugar, but we know no more than
that. The *Mary Russell* left Bridgetown,
Barbados, for Cork on 9 May. Assuming the
passage out was the normal forty days or so,
she stayed in Bridgetown for about six weeks.
It could be that the mules took some time to
sell, or that the port was unusually busy and
everything took longer than anticipated. The
long stopover is unlikely, for economic
reasons, to have been planned in order to
allow the delicate boy, Thomas Hammond, to
benefit from the climate, but this was a
welcome side effect.

We know that the port was busy because
the *Mary Russell* spent part of her stay there
'rafted' to a brig of similar size, the *Mary*

Stubbs of New Brunswick, British North America, under Captain Robert Callendar. When ports were busy, ships were lashed or rafted together to save space. Sometimes the raft of ships was used as a bridge so that their crews could walk to and from the shore; sometimes there were just two or more ships sharing a mooring.

Captain Callendar was, like Captain Stewart, a family man in his fifties, and also a devout Protestant who insisted on high standards aboard — no grog for the men, and no cursing. The two men agreed on many topics, and spent many hours sitting on the quarterdeck of one boat or the other as the sun was going down, sharing a tot of rum, and putting the world to rights.

It was part of Captain Stewart's responsibility, with the help of a shipping agent, to sell the mules for the best possible price, and secure a lucrative cargo for the homebound voyage. This he did, investing the income from the mules in 'Sugar, hides and other produce of the island, to the value, exclusive of duty, of about £4000'. That was a lot of money, considering that the boat itself was worth £1,200, but it no doubt included the profit that would be made when it was sold on the Cork market. Dark brown Muscovado sugar from Barbados was highly prized for the moistness and distinctive flavour that came from its high molasses content. In 1828 sugar cane was still processed on Barbados by slave labour, which was not finally abolished until 1834. Rum, highly potent and much prized by seafarers, was a by-product of the sugar industry.

The Muscovado sugar was transported in wooden barrels known, to indicate their size, as hogsheads and tierces. The crew would contrive to pack as many barrels as possible into the hold of the *Mary Russell*, filling the gaps between barrels with the hides.

The only incident during the *Mary Russell*'s stay in Barbados on record is that Smith incurred his captain's wrath by staying on shore overnight. In Smith's own words: 'While in Barbados I slept out only one night. The Captain was angry for it and said I was a pretty pattern for the men.' He was, presumably, at a brothel. Stewart saw this as a bad example for the young men and boys aboard.

While in Barbados, the *Mary Russell* was approached by a Cork man, Captain James Goold Raynes. Raynes had shipped out of Cove on the same day as Captain Stewart, as captain of the *Hibernia*. But according to Scoresby, 'he had been deprived of his command on account of a recent habit of intemperance', that is, he had been demoted from captain owing to drunkenness. So he was stranded in Bridgetown. Finding the *Mary Russell* about to leave for Cork, Raynes asked for a passage home, and was immediately refused. His reputation for drunkenness had preceded him. But, Scoresby tells us, when Captain Stewart found out that Raynes could not get a passage on any other boat, he took pity on him, gave in to his repeated request, 'and kindly permitted him to embark in the brig for Cork'. Little did either man suspect the fatal consequences of this kind gesture.

The *Mary Russell* finally sailed for Cork under a deep blue sky with a freshening wind to speed her on her way. As they waved goodbye to the crew aboard the *Mary Stubbs*, which was not due to sail for another day, the captain, crew and passengers had every reason to expect an uneventful seven-week trip. The list of people on board was the same as for the voyage out, with the addition of Captain James Raynes, travelling as a passenger, as were the ostlers, Timothy Connell and James Morley.

Their course home would differ from the one taken out, according to Ron Holland, yacht designer and enthusiast of marine history, because of the prevailing winds. They would return by picking up the Gulf Stream, sailing between Cuba and Florida and up the coast of North America, before picking up a westerly wind to blow them home. The voyage home, at an average of about fifty days, was generally about ten days longer than the voyage out.

Captain Raynes had been allocated a berth off the main cabin, next door to the captain's, while the boy Thomas Hammond had his day and night bed in the main cabin. As on the way out, Smith slept in the berth next to the captain's. The ostlers Connell and Morley were to share the men's quarters in the fo'c'sle. Although nominally passengers, Connell and Morley regularly helped to work the ship, including steering and working aloft with the sails, either as a refuge from boredom or as a way of acquiring new skills. We know that Timothy Connell was twenty-eight at the time, and Morley might have been around the same age. Raynes was described by John Howes as 'a quiet, inoffensive gentleman, who was very obliging and assisted in working the vessel'. He washed and shaved with the crew, and while doing so often chipped in *as Gaeilge* while the men were talking among themselves. The ostler James Morley had grown up speaking Irish, and his English was very poor.

About ten days after they had set sail, according to Scoresby,

Captain Stewart began to harbour a strong and increasing suspicion of a mutiny being meditated on the part of his passenger, Raynes, and some of his crew. This suspicion seems first to have been excited by a dream, which, on a mind naturally and habitually superstitious, had a very powerful effect. He communicated the circumstance to his chief mate, William Smith, observing that God Almighty had warned him in a dream that Raynes meditated his destruction and the seizure of the vessel, in order to avoid the mortification of returning to a port where he had ceased to be respected, and from whence he has no longer the expectation of obtaining a command.

Smith expressed surprise at the captain's certainty of a mutinous plot. He had not observed anything unusual taking place before the mast. The crew aboard the *Mary Russell* was one of the best he had ever been to sea with, and he had a long and varied career behind him. The practical-minded Scotsman told his captain 'It was a folly to mind dreams, they were false.'

Shortly after Captain Stewart had confided

the prophetic dream to his chief mate, William Smith in turn made a confession to Stewart, concerning an episode earlier in his naval career. Smith told his captain about an incident aboard a frigate of the Royal Navy, in which he had taken part in the murder of a marine, while anchored off the Downs (a sheltered anchorage between the mouth of the Thames and Dover), and successfully escaped detection. He had got away with murder.

We can only speculate as to what caused Smith to make this confession, but it was a bad move. He was ordered to leave his comfortable bunk and sleep in the half-deck. His place was taken by second mate, William Swanson, who had previously been banished from the cabin, before the brig had left Cove. From that point on Captain Stewart ceased to trust Smith, and treated him with increasing suspicion. As Scoresby put it, his prophetic dream had given Stewart 'a jaundiced eye', and he started to see perfectly innocent conduct and ordinary events as confirmation of a mutiny being plotted.

The next man to arouse the captain's ire was Captain Raynes. Scoresby tells the story:

Among the early occurrences after this dream, which excited his observation, was the circumstance of Raynes associating a good deal with the crew, to whose compartment of the vessel he was in the habit of retiring to shave himself, and with some of whom he was occasionally heard conversing in Irish, a language which Stewart did not understand. This, under the influence of awakened suspicion, annoyed the Captain greatly, and he seriously remonstrated with his passenger upon the impropriety of his conduct; but it does not appear that he afterwards gave any real occasion for complaint, either in this or in any other respect.

The captain had become so convinced of the impending mutiny that he ordered Frank Sullivan, one of the younger sailors, and Timothy Connell, whom he liked and trusted, to sleep in the great cabin outside his berth. Even so, he hardly slept at all. He had become unusually pale, and was losing weight. For his personal defence he armed himself with a harpoon, the carpenter's axe, a heavy, trident-like instrument called a granes, and a crowbar. Scoresby again:

His conduct now became more and more particular [odd]. He was agitated, watchful, and increasingly suspicious. He ordered the mate to walk the deck armed with the granes and a knife. He took alarm from the most trifling circumstances. The seaman Howes having asked for instructions as to the method of taking lunar observations, with which the Captain was very familiar, excited the apprehension that he wished for this knowledge for a bad purpose.

At the moment, the only person on board who could navigate by the stars was the captain. If Howes were to learn this art, the captain would become dispensable, and mutiny would be an ever more tempting prospect, according to Captain Stewart's 'jaundiced eye'. A few days later, Keating, who was steering, innocently asked Captain Stewart whether Captain Raynes was a good navigator. This convinced Stewart that the crew were measuring Raynes up with a view to having him as their future commander.

About half-way home, Stewart's suspicions of his crew's planned mutiny had reached such a height that he called all hands aft and told them that because of Howes' interest in mastering lunar navigation, and Keating's inquiry about Captain Raynes's navigational skills, he had strong reason to believe that they were making plans to harm him and take control of the ship.

The men, greatly surprised that their captain should hold such suspicions, protested their innocence, and declared their loyalty to him as master of the brig. Captain Stewart found their surprise genuine, and was reassured by their expressions of loyalty. His confidence in the crew was restored far enough to relieve him of suspicion for a few days. But little by little, his anxiety and watchfulness returned. Against all logic, suspicion took over again. Once more he became convinced that the crew were conspiring to overpower him in the night while he slept, and take possession of the ship. He decided that in addition to having armed himself as best he could and appointed bodyguards to sleep in the main cabin, he would make the prospect of mutiny less attractive by jettisoning most of the navigation equipment.

In order that this gesture should have the fullest possible impact on the crew, he called the chief mate William Smith, Captain Raynes and the boy John Deaves into the main cabin. He promised to show them something that they had never seen before.

Then, after charging Raynes with speaking Irish, as a proof of a design to corrupt the crew, he ordered the log-reel and sand-glasses to be thrown overboard through the cabin window, which was done. Afterwards he threw his box of charts overboard, observing, in reply to a remark of the mate, 'They are my own, and I can make more.' And lastly, he openly tore the leaves out of the log-book, commanding his officers, as they stood by in amazement, not to keep any more reckoning.

Without the log, they had no accurate record of the ship's position on its long passage from Barbados to Cove. Captain Stewart's intention was that the absence of navigational equipment would act as a deterrent to mutiny, as the sailors would have no idea of their position, thus rendering them liable to become lost at sea. However, he had not been totally honest in his dramatic gesture, as he admitted to William Scoresby:

He had a sufficient and secret reserve, as he himself afterwards told me, of a log-glass and some spare line, the last leaf of the log-book, and also a chart belonging to Captain Raynes, which he secreted under his bed, lest he should afterwards get into difficulty of the destruction of property not his own. With these things in reserve, therefore, he had the means, as occasion might enable him to employ them, for keeping an imperfect kind of reckoning from day to day. Being himself, however, an expert navigator, he relied chiefly, for the determination of the position of the ship, on celestial observations, which he continued sedulously at every opportunity to take and calculate, up to the very day preceding the final catastrophe.

The jettisoning of the navigation equipment had one further witness, eleven-year-old Thomas Hammond, who was on his day bed in the main cabin while this dramatic gesture was made. Thomas Hammond had known Captain Stewart all his life. He had noticed a big change in Captain Stewart since they had started the passage home. On the way out, Captain Stewart was quite pleasant, the same man he had known at home. But on the way back, he had confided his suspicions of Captain Raynes to the child, and frequently told him about his dreams of Captain Raynes taking over the ship. Captain Stewart was different now, pale and nervous, never taking off his clothes to go to sleep. He hardly slept at all, and when he was awake he had strange, glittering eyes that were frightening. And now he had thrown all the navigation instruments overboard, and torn up the log. Captain Stewart was acting more like a madman every day. Thomas Hammond began to suspect that he might never see his home again.

5

The Tying up of the First Mate

Thanks to Captain Stewart's daily calculations, the ship continued sailing on its correct course, bringing it ever closer to the south coast of Ireland. As they reached more northerly latitudes the men once more donned their heavier gear. When they turned west for Ireland, the weather became milder, but even so the June weather in the North Atlantic felt chilly after the heat of Barbados. Their captain continued to be persistently watchful, and remained distant from his men. The easy companionship that had prevailed on the outward voyage, in spite of the encumbrance of a cargo of mules, had evaporated. Stewart was on his nerve ends, jumpy and tense: he hardly ate, and seldom slept more than a couple of hours at a stretch. His previously benign expression was replaced with a frown, his face was pale, his eyes strangely bright. Even the smallest departure from the normal ship's routine caused him to start in alarm. John Howes noticed that often, when speaking to the men, Stewart would wander from one subject to another, and give ridiculous explanations for his conduct.

At some point before Wednesday 18 June (testimony on exactly when is contradictory and imprecise), most likely the very day before, a ship sailed into sight. She was the *Mary Harriet*, travelling from New York to Liverpool. Captain Stewart signalled his intentions of coming aboard, and both brigs hove-to, while the boat was lowered from the *Mary Russell*. Captain Stewart took with him Francis Sullivan, who had become a great friend and whom he had been instructing in basic navigation, one other man, and the boy Richards.

We do not know what Captain Stewart told the captain of the *Mary Harriet*, but presumably he shared his suspicions of a mutinous plot on board, for the *Mary Harriet's* captain loaned him a brace of pistols. He concealed these, not wanting his crew to know he now had firearms. He also came back with beef and pork, to bolster their supplies, and they resumed their journey.

During the night of Wednesday 18–19 June, the chief mate, Smith, was in charge of the middle watch. Soon after he went on deck he needed to go down to the nail locker, which was situated in the passage to the cabin, to fetch oil for the binnacle lamp (the lamp that lit the binnacle, a protective box in which the compass was suspended), which seemed to be running out. After a very short interval, the light again became dim, so he went down a second and then a third time to the nail locker to fetch implements for trimming the wick. Scoresby's account continues:

> The repeated footsteps of the mate in his passage to and fro, betwixt the deck and the steerage, were anxiously observed by the wakeful Captain, who, ignorant of the real cause, supposed that the midnight trespasser there must be in search of some deadly instrument, whereby to prosecute the suspected murderous purpose against himself.

In spite of his chronic insomnia, the captain must have nodded off, because it was morning before he took any action. Knowing that Smith had been in charge of the watch (Smith, who had admitted to getting away with murder), as soon as he got up he armed himself with a harpoon, went straight to the half-deck hatchway, the mate's sleeping place since he had been banished from the main cabin. When Captain Stewart called his name, Smith, who had headed straight for his hammock after finishing his watch, responded immediately. His enraged captain said: 'It's well for you, after the proceedings of last night, that you are in your rightful sleeping place. If I'd found you forward among the crew, I would have put you to death as a mutineer.'

Smith, who had once been the captain's trusted friend, expressed great surprise at this sudden accusation, and his surprise turned to alarm when he was threatened with the harpoon, which the captain was pointing at his breast. The captain shouted again, accusing him of being the ringleader of the mutiny.

The rest of the crew had already been alerted by the raised voices, and now gathered around the hatchway at their captain's summons.

'Is it not true, Smith is the leader?' The captain continued to poke the harpoon at the chest of Smith, who had leapt out of his hammock at the first threat of assault. 'Smith is the leader of the mutiny, is he not?'

Speaking at first all at once, the crew members attempted to reassure their captain that there was no mutiny.

'Tell me the truth,' he asked again. 'I am convinced that my suspicions are correct. There is a mutinous plot afoot aboard this ship. Every last man of you is involved.'

Once again the crew chorused their denial of his suspicions, each swearing to the innocence of his shipmates.

Then they spoke to him individually, led by the second mate William Swanson, who reassured the captain in his heavy Swedish accent that there was no mutiny aboard, and that Smith was no ringleader. The most senior among them, Howes, spoke next, his voice warm with genuine affection, stemming from the hurt he felt at the unfairness of the accusation.

'We wouldn't harm a hair on your head, Captain Stewart, that is God's honest truth,' he said.

His sentiments were echoed in turn by the carpenter, John Cramer, Francis Sullivan and John Keating. Then the senior apprentice John Deaves, shaking his head, reassured his captain that there was no mutiny, while Daniel Scully and Henry Richards stood beside him, backing up his words. The passengers, Captain Raynes, Timothy Connell and James Morley, who had been included in the accusation of mutiny, joined in the chorus of denials.

All on board watched in silence as the captain suddenly let fall the harpoon he had been pointing at Smith, and stared around at them with tears pouring down his face. He was deeply touched by the honest declarations of his sailors, and convinced by the sincerity with which they denied the charge that he must have been mistaken about the mutinous plot. He shook hands with them, one by one, starting with second mate Swanson, and ending with the boy Henry Richards.

'You are all honest men,' he said, looking directly at the group of sailors above him on deck. The tears had dried up, and now his eyes were strangely glittering. 'You are all honest men', he repeated in a more aggressive tone of voice, 'except for the mate, William Smith. Seize him, and tie him up!'

Smith had joined his companions on deck, and started back at the new order. Nobody moved to obey the captain, so he repeated his words in a furious roar, addressing himself this time directly to Captain Raynes: 'In the name of King George IV, seize the mate and tie him up!'

Still no one moved. 'But the mate's done nothing wrong,' said Howes. 'I don't see anything the matter with the mate.'

Then Sullivan spoke: 'If we lash the mate without reason, he will take the law on us when we get home.'

The voices of Swanson, Cramer and

Keating were raised in agreement, restating the two facts: the mate had done nothing wrong, and if they tied him up without good reason, he could bring the law on them back in port. Unwilling to obey the order, the men turned as one, and walked away from the captain and the first mate.

The effect of this mass resistance to his will had an instant impact on the captain. To see the whole ship's company actively disobeying what he saw as a necessary order, sent him into a great rage. He became greatly agitated, pacing the quarterdeck in double-quick time. Before coming up to remonstrate with Smith he had put the recently acquired pistols in his pockets, and now he brought them out for all to see. His pale face had turned purple, and his hands were trembling with the strength of his emotion. The men watched him, frightened at what they saw. If the captain came to harm, then who would guide the boat home to port?

William Swanson, John Keating and Timothy Connell were so alarmed by their captain's rage that they pleaded with Smith to let himself be bound in the hope of returning the ship to a more normal state and getting home safely. Once they were back in port, the three men promised they would bear witness for him and swear that he had committed no crime. Once they were all safely ashore, the captain would feel the strength of the law, they assured him. Smith, who was also alarmed at the captain's rage, reluctantly agreed:

Approaching his agitated commander, the yielding officer presented his united hands, and accosted him, saying, 'Here! Tie away!' His hands were accordingly secured; and he then retired, in submission to the captain's orders, into the lazarette, a compartment beneath the cabin floor.

The lazarette was to the aft of the main cabin, and was used for storing spare line and cables, blocks, fenders and other gear that was seldom needed at sea. When loading the cargo, the men had put some of the hides in the lazarette, and this was what Smith found himself lying on. It was a black, almost airless hole, rank with the hides' animal odour. Smith lay on his back with his tied hands in front of him, and shuffled his body from side to side in the narrow space, trying to find the least uncomfortable position.

Smith had just come off watch, and had not had a chance to eat anything. Having submitted to being tied in spite of not having committed any crime, it seemed to him an additional punishment to be deprived of food, and he complained loudly of having missed breakfast. Captain Stewart, ever a fair and kind captain, ordered that breakfast (porridge and hot tea) be brought to him in the lazarette, and fed to him by Frank Sullivan. This strange process was watched with interest from his day bed in the cabin by the boy Thomas Hammond, who had listened to every word of the discussions on deck through the cabin's open skylight.

6

The Tying up of the Crew

Captain Stewart was awoken from a light sleep on Friday morning by Smith calling from the lazarette for a drink of water. He had a quick look at him and inspected his bonds, confirming that they were still secure. Smith begged for the bonds to be loosed, as he was already a prisoner, and complained that he was suffocating from lack of air. Stewart refused to loosen his bonds, but sent the carpenter, John Cramer, to make an air hole in the planks above the lazarette so that Smith could breathe more easily. Then he ordered Francis Sullivan to bring the mate a drink of water.

As they sailed along with a fair wind, and fine, clear weather, Captain Stewart spent all Friday thinking of a way to tie up the other nine men. He had decided that this was the only way he could bring the ship safely into port. None of the men was to be trusted: they were all potential mutineers. He could not overpower them by direct attack. What he could do was outwit them, trick them into

71

being tied up. Once they were secure, he could sail the boat single-handed with the help of the boys, and bring them all safely home.

Apart from the whimperings of the imprisoned Smith, an unusual hush had fallen over the brig, with none of the usual banter coming from the fo'c'sle. Everyone was tense, and silent, as if knowing something momentous was about to happen. Captain Raynes moved his gear from the main cabin to the fo'c'sle, telling John Howes that 'from him and Captain Stewart not agreeing, he would come forward and remain there'.

At noon on Saturday 21 June, Captain Stewart took his last observation. The brig had reached the latitude of 50° North, longitude, 19° 50′ West, about 400 miles west-southwest of Cape Clear. As he was going below to put away his instrument and tables, he summoned John Deaves, Daniel Scully and Henry Richards to the cabin. Captain Stewart went into his berth, and took his pistols from their case, placing one in each pocket. Then he called the boys to his berth, and closed the door in order to speak to them privately. It was a tight fit, the three boys sitting on the berth with their knees under their chins, and the captain standing on the narrow strip of floor.

Captain Stewart repeated his belief in the intended mutiny. Then he pulled a pistol out of his right pocket, and threatened the boys with instant death in the event of their betraying him. He pointed the pistol first at John Deaves, poking him in the chest between his knees, then did the same to Daniel Scully, and finally Henry Richards. He spoke clearly and intensely in a low voice, explaining that if they did not obey his orders unquestioningly, and refrain from all communication with the rest of the crew, they would be shot dead. They promised him their loyalty, as they had done two days earlier when the whole ship's crew had been accused of mutiny.

Captain Stewart then changed his tone of voice to a more familiar and friendly one. If they stayed loyal to him, they would become rich men, because Lloyds, the insurers of the ship and its cargo, would be so grateful to them for having helped to prevent the mutiny which would lead to the loss of both, that they would each receive valuable rewards, enough money to turn themselves into gentlemen. All they had to do was sign the piece of paper that he handed them, confirming that there was a mutiny aboard. They signed, eyeing the captain's pistols warily. Then he put his fingers to his lips, and dismissed them from his berth.

As they passed through the cabin on their way to the companionway that led to the deck, they moved with a new slowness and sense of purpose, as if a huge burden had been put on their shoulders. Not one of them stopped to have a word with Thomas Hammond who was dreaming on his day bed, wondering why the Captain had had this hushed exchange in his cabin with the three boys, and wondering how long he would have to listen to the moanings and whimperings of Smith from the lazarette in the cabin floor. Everything was getting very strange; the whole ship's routine, always comfortingly predictable, seemed to young Hammond to be falling apart.

They were steering under full sail with a following wind for the southwest coast of Ireland. Before Captain Stewart could begin to carry out his plan, he needed to reduce sail in order to be able to handle the boat on his own. He ordered the headsails to be furled, and the main topsail to be close reefed. These were extraordinary orders to give on a brig heading home in fair weather, at a point where they would normally want to make all possible speed. But the crew were not inclined to question his order, nor indeed to disobey it, after the display of rage that their refusal to tie up Smith had provoked. Swanson, Howes and the apprentice John Deaves were on deck, with Sullivan at the wheel. Sullivan put the ship head into the wind, and Captain Stewart asked Captain Raynes if he would help to bring in the sail. He agreed immediately.

William Scoresby, in a section entitled 'Device for Securing the Crew', gives a detailed description of the cabin of the *Mary Russell* to enable us to understand how Captain Stewart's plan worked.

The cabin measured about 12 feet across, by 8 or 9 feet fore and aft, and the height was about 5 feet 10 inches clear of the beams of the upper deck. The entrance to the cabin was by a staircase on the larboard [port] side of the quarter deck, shielded by a small 'companion' opening towards the stern, and situated far aft, very near the taff rail [which stood on the stern of the boat]. Such was the position and construction of the companion, that no person on the main-deck, or forward, or aloft in the rigging, could perceive anything that was going on in the cabin.

The cabin was lit by two large windows in the stern of the boat, and by a small skylight in the quarterdeck. On each side of the cabin was an open berth, one of which, on the starboard side, was occupied by the boy Hammond. At the forward part of the cabin, near the sides, were entrances into the master's and mate's berths.

While Captain Raynes, Swanson, Howes and Deaves were reducing sail, the rest of the men, Keating, Cramer, and the ostlers Timothy Connell and James Morley, were eating in the fo'c'sle. When they finished, Timothy Connell, as was his custom, took a walk on deck.

Standing at the top of the companionway, Captain Stewart summoned Connell down. He addressed Connell familiarly as Timothy; he was officially a passenger, not a crew member, and the captain had befriended him. As Connell was regularly asked to act as a bodyguard to the captain, he would have had no reason to suspect anything out of the ordinary in this call. Scoresby continues:

A far different reception from what he had imagined awaited him there. A pistol was pointed to his breast by the hand of his now resolute Captain, who called upon him: 'Confess the truth, or I will blow your brains out!' Then, under the charge of being a party in an intended mutiny, which his confused and alarmed manner was considered as verifying, he was ordered, by directions given to one of the boys, to be forthwith bound. Fearing the consequences of a refusal, before one so armed and apparently so determined, Connell submitted; and when properly secured, he was forthwith removed into one of the interior cabins, out of sight.

Next the captain sent Deaves on deck to summon seaman John Keating. He too suspected nothing out of the usual until he was confronted by 'a brace of pistols clapped to his head'. Charged with mutiny, like Connell before him, he was ordered, 'under penalty of instant death, to submit to being bound'. He to was securely tied, first by the boys, then more effectually by the captain, and dragged into an interior berth.

Then the boy Richards was sent to summon Captain Raynes, who submitted to the same procedure. Scoresby observes that the fact that 'Captain Stewart was in the habit of tying his men as a punishment', and that his repeated assurances that if they agreed quietly to be bound, no further harm would come to them, were another reason why nobody raised the alarm. The chief reason was that they had a loaded pistol pointed at them. He continues:

In this manner, with scarcely a single varying circumstance, and without exciting either alarm or suspicion in the breasts of those who remained behind, no less than six out of the eight men, to whose liberty the scheme extended, were successfully assailed.

Connell, Keating, Raynes, Swanson, Cramer and Sullivan were called in succession at intervals of fifteen to twenty minutes, and tied up.

Chief mate William Smith, lying below the floor on which the captain and the boys were tying up the men, was a witness to the procedures. From the moment that he had heard Captain Stewart threaten to shoot Timothy Connell, Smith had stopped moaning, and writhed in silence as he tried to find a bearable position in which to lie. He could not see what was going on, but he could hear. He knew that only Morley and Howes remained at liberty. James Morley, the ostler, was just a landsman and not likely to resist, but John Howes would not give in easily. The only hope that Smith could see of Captain Stewart's plan being confounded lay with the redoubtable John Howes.

The boy Thomas Hammond watched everything from his day bed, cowering back against the wood panelling behind him, for he had never before been in the same room as a loaded pistol. And this loaded pistol was in the hands of a man that Hammond had already decided was mad: Captain Stewart, who had once been like a father to him, was quite mad, not in his right mind, as mad as any lunatic in the Cork Asylum.

Captain Stewart decided to deal with Howes next, and sent one of the boys to summon him. Howes knew that the rest of the crew were below in the cabin with the captain, and he assumed that his summons meant that the captain was having another attack of doubt about the loyalty of his crew, and wished to address the ship's company once more on that topic. He was even hoping there might be a tot of rum once the captain got over his notions and they were all friends again. When he got to the top of the companionway, Howes called down to the captain and asked whether he was wanted below. That answer was yes, so Howes swung himself down the companionway, but missed his footing and slipped down a couple of steps. He came to a halt less than halfway down, and was riveted to the spot by a loud cry: 'Avast! Not so fast!' Howes turned to see

79

his captain at the foot of the stairs, his pistols cocked in his hands.

Howes ignored the fact that a mere pull of the trigger lay between life and death, and asked: 'What do you intend to do with your pistols?'

'I have found you out,' was the answer. 'I have heard all,' (implying that the other men had confessed that Howes was a leader of the mutiny). Howes turned suddenly and started climbing up the staircase again, at which the captain 'snapped two pistols at him', but they failed to fire. Howes raced back up the ladder, and called down to his captain: 'Remember, you snapped two pistols at me, and I'll have satisfaction when we get to Cork, if it costs me my life!'

The captain, pistols still in hand, chased Howes up on deck, shouting, 'I'll satisfy you, I'll give you satisfaction . . . ' He cocked one of his pistols again, and shot at the retreating seaman, but missed him. Before he could get the other pistol ready, Howes had reached the fo'c'sle and jumped down the open hatchway, grabbing Morley and pushing him ahead of him into the shadows at the side of the ship. The captain stopped at the hatchway, and retreated, being wary of finding himself at a disadvantage in the darkness below with two men on the loose.

Having failed to constrain Howes by trickery and by force of arms, Captain Stewart decided to try to talk the seaman into surrendering. He chose to argue Howes into submission, knowing that the unusually intelligent seaman enjoyed using his wits. First he tried threats, declaring that as captain of the ship, he was morally justified in shooting anyone who opposed his will. If he could not shoot Howes, then he would brand him as a ringleader in the mutiny, and bring him to justice. Howes merely repeated his assertion that he knew of no mutiny on board, and was not a ringleader of any kind.

Then the captain tried an appeal to Howes' better feelings.

Lamenting that he had had no rest for several nights previous, the Captain earnestly entreated him to submit, pledging his word that no harm should accrue to him, and piteously urging that 'if they were all tied, then he might get sleep, and all would be well again'.

The ploy worked, and the soft-hearted Howes agreed to be tied. He still protested at the undeserved punishment, but to prove his innocence of the accusation of mutiny, and to prove that he feared neither the threatened bondage nor having to face a charge of mutiny, he asked Morley to tie his hands behind him, then made his way up on deck. There the captain re-secured his hands, and tied his feet together. When Howes complained at this extreme form of bondage, Stewart justified himself by saying that 'Captain Raynes and Timothy Connell had acknowledged their piratical intentions'. Howes continued to protest his ignorance of any plot,

... and called on his master, if he thought him guilty and deserving of death, to shoot him at once. The Captain applauded his bravery, and added 'that he had no wish to injure him; for it was his anxious desire to take him, above all others on board, with a whole skin to Cork'.

Then he searched Howes and confiscated his knife, and called Morley, the last of the victims, to come up from the fo'c'sle and be tied. Morley submitted.

The entire crew (apart from the apprentices) and all the passengers (bar the boy Hammond) were now in a state of helpless bondage. The boys could be seen occasionally by Howes, pacing the deck, armed with the harpoon, the axe and the granes.

Having tied Howes and Morley on deck,

Captain Stewart began a systematic survey of the condition of each of the tied men. John Keating had fainted, so Stewart untied his arms and legs, and led him up on to the deck, where he tied him to the staple of the companionway. Keating, Howes and Morley were all in the open air, on the after part of the deck, a few feet away from each other.

Howes, with characteristic hardihood and recklessness, solicited the boon of a pipe of tobacco, which, being prepared for him, and put into this mouth, he contrived to retain between his lips and smoke.

Daniel Scully was put on guard duty watching the prisoners on deck, while the captain continued his inspection of his prisoners below deck. Having so recently left a tropical climate, the three men on deck soon became chilled by the night air. When they complained of the cold, the captain, with considerable effort, dragged Keating and Morley into the cabin. But he dared not risk putting Howes in with the rest of the men because of his determined and outspoken character. Instead he left Howes on the after-hatch and covered him with a blanket. Howes continued to complain loudly of the cold, and eventually the captain gave the boys permission to help Howes move into the half-deck — the former berth of the mate, William Smith — where he would be more sheltered.

By now, night had fallen. After about three hours on his own, wrapped in his blanket, Howes was woken by the captain and one of the boys. The boy held a lantern, while the captain tightened the prisoner's fastenings. They were so uncomfortable, cutting into his flesh and hindering his circulation, that Howes declared he could not live another hour in such a state. The captain tried to calm him down, addressing him familiarly as 'John'. He joked with him about the distress of two of the prisoners in the cabin, saying that their terror at their situation seemed to contradict their declarations of innocence. The captain thought it was a rather good joke, and repeated it to Howes, who did not find it funny: 'If they were innocent, they ought not to be afraid,' repeated the captain. Promising to return in about an hour, he then left Howes alone to his suffering.

Howes did not mind being alone, but he objected strongly to being tied up so painfully. He had agreed to be tied: why could he not therefore be tied reasonably, so that he was not in pain? The angrier he became, the more effort and ingenuity he put into trying to loosen his bonds. He struggled and squirmed and let the bonds chafe his skin until he bled in the hope that the accumulated movements would loosen the ropes. Soon he was rewarded by being able to free one of his hands. He stretched and clenched the fingers to revive his circulation, then used his free hand to loosen the bonds on the other. As he did so, he vowed that never again would he let himself be tied, even if death were the only alternative. Having gained access to shelter from the cold, and loosened his bonds, Howes passed a reasonably comfortable night.

This was not the case with his unfortunate shipmates in the main cabin. On first being tied, they had all been quietly resigned to their fate, assuming it would be of short duration, and not too uncomfortable. But Captain Stewart's second round of tightening led to an increase in pain, amounting to 'absolute torture'.

Captain Stewart was unaffected by the cries of pain and alarm that issued every time a man struggled to find a more bearable position. Daniel Scully had managed to place a thin mattress under Captain Raynes, but nevertheless every muscle in his body cried out with pain. However, he was the only one who did not utter a single cry of complaint.

The hands of the carpenter, John Cramer, had become shockingly inflamed, and he seemed on the point of fainting from the pain, so Captain Stewart released the tension of the cord on his wrists ever so slightly, until his hands returned to a less alarming shade of red. Stewart sat himself down in the chair that was built into the port berth of the great cabin, and prepared to watch over his crew, while the boys were sent to the fo'c'sle for some much-needed rest.

William Smith, lying in his lazarette, was hungry and thirsty, as well as in pain, but he did not dare call out in case the captain decided to tighten his bonds. He writhed about, aware that he was lying on part of the cargo of hides, trying to find a less agonising position. Occasionally he let out a whimper, knowing that it would not be heard above the moans and cries of the seven other bound men in the cabin.

On his day bed opposite the captain's chair, the delicate boy, Thomas Hammond, wrapped himself in his blanket, pulling it right over his head to muffle the moans of his shipmates, and prayed very hard, harder than he had ever prayed before in his short life. The brig, meanwhile, continued lying-to in the dark, under a very low sail, with the helm lashed a-lee.

7

Howes' Escape

At daybreak on Sunday morning the boys were called up to the main cabin, and found the seven prisoners lying there as they had left them the previous evening. Captain Stewart was jittery after a sleepless night, wracked by doubts and panic, in case his men should somehow escape and take their revenge on him. He needed to tie them up even more securely, so that he could rest and relieve his tormented mind. He took spare rope from the downhaul of the mainsail, which was about the thickness of a man's index finger. He carefully constructed seven grommets — circles of rope — calculated to be just big enough to pass over a man's head. Then he drove large staples (or spikes where there was not enough room for a staple) into the deck of the cabin, one near the neck and one at the feet of each individual. Passing the circle of rope over the head of each prisoner, as far as the neck, he tied the underneath of it to the staple in the deck, so that no one could move from his place without suffocating.

Next, to prevent accidental strangulation, he passed a thick cord from the upper part of the grommet, near the chin, to the lower part of the body, which, on being drawn tight, pulled the grommet down towards the chest. Then he used new rope, which had been intended for a lead-line, to pinion the prisoners' arms to their bodies, and then tie up their legs and arms. Scoresby sums up the end result of Stewart's ropemanship:

The neck, by means of the grommet enveloping it, was fastened down to a staple. The arms were first pinioned behind, and then the hands were lashed together across the breast, the end of the cord used for this purpose being subsequently carried downward to the thighs. The thighs were then lashed together about their middle; another portion of the lashing went around the ankles; and ultimately, the extremity of the cord was firmly secured to the foot-staple, or nail, driven into the deck. And for the more effectual security of the lashings, those on the limbs were 'frapped' or twitched together, by cross lashing; and where any ends of the cords appeared in sight, these were usually 'seized' together with twine or rope yarn, to prevent their being unloosed.

Captain Stewart considered it a fine, seamanlike job. This operation had taken the captain and the boys, who did the frapping and seizing, some hours to complete, during which the men had made various proposals for regaining their freedom. With one exception, the crew were willing to be cast adrift in an open boat, knowing they were only about 300 miles off land. The exception was the chief mate, who could hear the discussion from the lazarette, and was consulted at intervals by the others on the conditions of their release. Under no circumstances was William Smith prepared to quit the *Mary Russell* until she reached port. To do so would, to his mind, have been an admission of guilt, and lead to him being labelled a mutineer, a crime of which he was innocent.

Captain Stewart offered his crew the longboat with provisions, compass, sails and everything else they needed to reach land safely. Once they were off the brig, he need have no fear that they were planning to murder him and seize the ship. But there was one problem: he was not prepared to free more than one man to help with hoisting out the boat (which usually needed at least three strong men), and he did not consider that he himself, one able bodied seaman and the boys would be strong enough to hoist the boat successfully and get her afloat. The carpenter, John Cramer, agreed that one man would not be enough, and pleaded with him to release two men. But the captain held firm: only one man would be released to help hoist the boat. His unspoken fear was that two men would gang up on him and overpower him. Captain Stewart's dilemma was compounded by the fact that the mate, Smith, would not agree to go with the men in the longboat. Even though he was securely tied in the lazarette, Stewart would not rest a minute if Smith were left on board with himself and the boys. The problem of Smith and the impossibility of launching the longboat with the help of only one man led Stewart to abandon that plan.

As far as Stewart could see, unless a passing vessel came to his rescue, his only plan of action was to keep his prisoners securely tied up. He was satisfied that those in the cabin could not free themselves from their bondage, but he had one major concern: John Howes, whom he had left alone in the half-deck the previous evening.

At about ten o'clock on Sunday morning Captain Stewart and the three boys went looking for John Howes. The captain had his pistols primed, and he had armed Deaves with a harpoon, Scully with a granes and

Richards with the carpenter's axe. They followed behind him in single file, reluctant to appear as enemies to John Howes who had always treated them kindly. The captain removed the hatch of the half-deck, which had not been moved since he closed it, and called out to his prisoner, whom he could just make out in the shadows under the side of the deck.

'John! Are you there? Are you tied? Turn your back that I may see.'

Howes turned himself cautiously, as little as he could, but enough for the quick, anxious eye of his captain to see that his bonds had been loosened:

Stewart ordered Howes to come forth under the hatchway to be better secured, threatening him, in the case of disobedience, with immediate death.

Howes refused, and once again denied any intention of mutiny. He said that the treatment he had already endured was 'worse than the Spanish rack,' and that 'sooner than he would submit to be so tied again, he would suffer death'.

Captain Stewart, leaning into the open hatchway, pointed his pistol at Howes and fiercely answered: 'Then I must shoot you, if you don't.'

'I see murder in your looks,' answered the determined sailor, 'but as I am the oldest of your crew, I shall be the least missed. Fire away! You're worse than a Turk or a Tartar or any other barbarian. You will yet meet a day [of reckoning] for this. Death is no terror to me, whatever it may be to the others.'

For a moment Howes' bravery, and the unfairness of his accusation stopped Stewart in his path. 'I am no barbarian.' he shouted. 'Have I not always been considered a humane man by those who sail with me?' Then he thrust his ready-charged pistol into the hatchway, aiming it at Howes. Howes stood square and unflinching, facing up to his aggressor. The captain pulled the trigger with an agitated, wavering hand, and missed. Another shot from the second pistol quickly followed, and struck the outstretched hand of the defenceless seaman, lodging in the fleshy part near the thumb. The captain was not sure of the extent of Howes' injury, but as his pistols were very small, and his victim remained standing, he reckoned he had not inflicted much damage. Captain Stewart quickly recharged his pistols for another attack. He fired for the third time, and the ball flew through Howes' jacket and grazed his side. He fell on his back, believing himself to be mortally wounded. The discharge of a fourth shot brought him back to consciousness, and he realised that the wound in his side was only minor. But he wanted the captain to give him up for dead, so he howled, 'You've shot me through the guts! I'm not long for this world,' and writhed as if in mortal agony, then fell back motionless as if he were dead.

The captain watched the drama anxiously, then turned and said to the three boys, 'He's dead.' In order to make sure that he was not being taken in by any temporary loss of consciousness or deliberate play-acting he ordered one of the boys to keep an eye on the hatchway, and let him know if Howes moved. 'He is quite dead,' was the boy's report.

This was the impression that the wounded sailor wished to convey. His only hope of escape depended on the captain believing he was dead. He managed to make it seem that the blood that was running from his wounded hand came from his body. When the captain returned to the hatchway and saw the blood seeping from Howes' inanimate body, he commented, 'He's got plenty of blood. He must soon be thrown overboard.'

Just after making this remark, the attention of the captain and his young helpers was distracted from Howes by the appearance of a sail on the western horizon. At last the much longed for ship was coming to Captain Stewart's rescue. He would be able to hand over his mutinous crew, and travel home safely to Cove. He ordered Scully to hoist the distress signal in the rigging. The vessel came near enough for him to see the captain on the quarterdeck, studying the decks of the *Mary Russell* through his telescope. Staring anxiously across the sea, willing the ship to change course with every fibre of his body, Captain Stewart explained to the boys, 'Almighty God has sent a ship to rid me of my people.' And sure enough, to prove that his words were true, and that Almighty God had indeed come to his rescue, the ship changed course and set sail to approach the *Mary Russell*. Captain Stewart smiled for the first time since the dream had warned him of the intended mutiny.

Time passed slowly as the ship crept nearer across the sea. Captain Stewart stood on his own quarterdeck then ran up and down the deck, waving frantically at this rescuer. He ordered his three boys to climb the rigging and attract the stranger's attention. The boat came close enough for Captain Stewart to cry out 'Ahoy there!' But at exactly the same moment, inexplicably, against the long-established custom of the seafaring community, the stranger bore away on a change of course. The boys came down from the rigging to see their captain distraught at this disappointment.

The distraction of the passing ship, and the sure knowledge that the boys would not be checking on him while she was approaching, gave John Howes a chance to ascertain the extent of his injuries. These were not as bad as he had feared, and he did not believe his life was in danger. But in his efforts to make sure he was not mortally injured, he had changed the position of his bleeding hand. This was noticed by one of the boys, and Howes, knowing that the boy knew he was not dead, sat up and looked around for some means of defence. At this very moment the captain looked into the hatchway. 'This fellow is not dead!' he cried, drawing his pistol and firing immediately at Howes. The ball lodged in his thigh, and Howes cried out on receiving the shot, 'That will do it.'

'No, it won't,' shouted his attacker, 'Your voice is too good. But I'll soon make it do.'

It was a moment of absolute terror for Howes. He was still partially fettered, his only free hand being the wounded one, but he was determined to resist the new attack. He used the few moments he had, while Captain Stewart reloaded his pistols, to make a desperate attempt to release his legs from their lashings. Having succeeded, he jumped to his feet, and in a moment more managed to release his other hand. He then positioned himself as well as he could between the deck and the cargo, to do battle for his life.

Calling on the boys, still armed with the harpoon (Deaves), the granes (Scully) and the axe (Richards), to follow, Captain Stewart led the way and jumped down the hatchway. The boys advanced warily to the attack. The only means of defence that Howes found to hand was a small packing case containing books that lay within his reach. He seized this and held it up to shield his body as he disappeared once more into the shadows at the side of the ship. It served its purpose, deflecting the ball, at which point, the captain roared encouragement to the apprentices: 'Strike, my brave boys! Push your harpoons into him!' As the boys hesitatingly threatened Howes, he pleaded to their better nature: 'Don't murder an innocent man. Don't let him lead you on, boys.' This brought Deaves and Scully to a halt, and they drew back. Deaves began to plead with the captain to spare John Howes, who was an innocent man. Both he and Scully were in tears.

This enraged the captain who turned on the boys: 'Do you want me to spare this man's life, and allow ourselves to be butchered? Go forward and fight, or I'll blow your brains out!' Once more, fear struck into the hearts of the young lads, not fear of the prospect of being wounded by John Howes, but fear of what their unpredictable commander might do next.

Howes, fuelled by adrenaline and desperation, took advantage of this stand-off between the captain and the boys to rush suddenly into the midst of his assailants, aiming for the victim in his sights, and seizing his astonished captain in his mighty grasp. The small, slightly built captain had a sudden surge of energy that enabled him for some moments to hold his own against the superior strength of his opponent. Somehow the captain managed to get Howes' finger stuck in his mouth, and bit on it so hard that he knocked out his front tooth, and broke Howes' finger. But Stewart could not last for long against the determination of a man fighting for his life. Within seconds, he staggered under the pressure of Howes' overpowering arm, dropped his charged pistol, and fell defenceless. Howes pinioned the captain to the deck by pressing his knee on his chest, and seized the harpoon with which the boy Deaves was half-heartedly threatening him. Armed with the harpoon, for a moment John Howes had the captain completely in his power, but the only way he could retain his supremacy was to kill him outright by thrusting the harpoon into his chest. Howes was a quick thinker, even in extremity, and he realised that if he, who had been charged with being the ringleader in a mutiny, should kill his captain, he would be assumed guilty, and his life would end in disgrace on the gallows. Howes' moment of hesitation allowed Richards to come to the rescue of his captain. Richards attacked Howes on the head with repeated blows of his axe. His efforts to avoid the axe blows forced Howes to let go of the captain, and as he did so he was blinded by streams of blood pouring down his face. The captain sprang aside, then fled the scene of bloodshed, followed by the three boys.

Howes was surprised and relieved to find himself alone in the fo'c'sle, even though he was severely wounded. He had come off better than he had expected. He wiped the blood from his eyes, and explored his head wounds with his hand. Still bleeding copiously, he retreated again into the darkness at the side of the ship, and with his little remaining strength crawled away across the barrels of sugar that formed the cargo, into the forepeak, where he remained hidden.

8

The Work of Death

The messy and inconclusive battle with John Howes left Captain Stewart in an even more agitated state of mind. Anxious that something might have gone amiss in his absence, he hurried back to his prisoners in the cabin, to examine their condition, and assure himself that they were still firmly bound. The tightness of their numerous lashings had left the men in a state of excruciating pain. They moaned loudly as they writhed in agony, trying to find relief from chafing bonds, cramp, hunger, thirst — the whole unprecedented ordeal of their long confinement. Hell could surely offer nothing worse.

Captain Stewart was deeply affected by his men's suffering. He tried to explain the severity of their confinement by referring again to their intended mutiny, his ears closed to their repeated claims of innocence. He called on his men to pray to God to send a ship their way, so that he could be relieved from having to look after so many prisoners, and they could be released from their painful ordeal. He became greatly distressed and anxious. He was mortified at being the instrument of so much suffering, but he could see no other way of ensuring safety from this mutinous crew. Then he threw himself on his knees amid his suffering men, with a prayer book in hand, and pleaded with God to deliver him from this terrible situation. The captain solemnly swore that if they would leave the ship, he would give them the longboat so that they could reach land. But once again, the voice of chief mate Smith from the lazarette protested that he would not leave the brig until it reached port, and the carpenter John Cramer asked again how they were to lower the boat without releasing more than one man. The rest of the men lay in despair and moaned ever louder as they realised that this escape route was not going to be followed.

Captain Stewart turned away from his contemplation of the suffering prisoners, and noticed the boy Richards standing near him, still holding the bloodied axe with which he had rescued the captain from the hands of John Howes. Captain Stewart felt a surge of affection for the young lad who had been, as he believed, the sole reason that he had escaped with his life from the clutches of Howes, the sole reason why Howes, having attacked his commander with the harpoon, was not now in charge of the ship. Stewart warmly praised the boy for his timely intervention, and kissed him affectionately on the cheek, as he would do a son of his own. Then he spoke to the boy with heartfelt gratitude: 'Henry Richards, you shall be rewarded by a hundred guineas for saving the ship, and be a gentleman all your life.'

Thomas Hammond, on his day bed, looked at Richards holding the bloodied axe and wondered what they had done to John Howes. The idea of good John Howes injured, or even dead, touched something in young Thomas Hammond that moved him deeply, and brought to his eye the first tear to be provoked by the long and terrible ordeal. John Howes was injured, probably dead: there was no hope now for the ship, everything had gone terribly wrong. The ship was as mad as its captain, and there was no hope at all that anything could be put right. Hammond pulled the blanket over his head again, and lay face down on his day bed so that Richards should not see him cry.

★ ★ ★

'Sail ahoy, sail ahoy!'
John Deaves and Daniel Scully came up on

deck while Captain Stewart was praising Richards, and had seen the sail from the quarterdeck. Deaves' call, as he was shinning up the rigging to get a better view, brought the captain and Richards on deck. The boat was to leeward, and no great distance away, sailing the same course as the *Mary Russell*. Captain Stewart attempted to intersect her course by trimming his scanty canvas. But the stranger was faster, and was outsailing her. Suddenly, to his great joy, the strange ship tacked, so that she was heading towards the *Mary Russell*. Captain Stewart ordered Scully to raise the distress signal, as before. On seeing this, the approaching brig hove-to, letting the *Mary Russell*, still under low sail, approach her. Captain Stewart was over-whelmed with relief. Almighty God had not failed him: he had sent another ship, and this one would surely rid him of his people, and bring an end to their terrible suffering. The two vessels were soon so close together that the waving of hats in one could be observed in the other. The three boys waved theirs for all they were worth. Even their commander, standing on the quarterdeck, removed his hat, and waved it at the stranger.

The stranger observed the *Mary Russell*, an apparently sound brig, no fault in the rudder, no fault in the rigging, listing neither to port nor starboard, travelling in a gentle breeze and fine weather yet with hardly any sail set, and became suspicious. What reason could there be for the signal of distress? Only one man could be seen on deck, and three boys. Where were the rest of the crew? The captain of the strange ship began to suspect that there might be pirates aboard the *Mary Russell*, attempting, by the distress signal, to decoy the unwary into boarding her. Rather than risk trouble at this stage in his passage, the stranger bore up, and sailed away from the brig.

Captain Stewart had been so sure that relief was at hand that a frenzy of desperation seized him when the second chance of rescue disappeared. He had been convinced that this was a case of Divine Providence coming to his rescue. God himself had sent this vessel to deliver him from his perilous condition. So when the ship turned away, he believed that Providence had not intended to rescue the ship. On the contrary, Providence was making a judgement against the prisoners. Providence was finding them guilty of mutiny. Captain Stewart already believed that two of his prisoners had admitted they were guilty of mutinous intentions; this abandonment of them by Providence in such unusual circum-stances — two ships in succession failing to respond to the distress signal — was proof of the guilt of them all.

So it was that, between 4 and 5 p.m. on Sunday 22 June, Captain Stewart decided he should carry out the judgment of God on all his prisoners by putting them to death. Up to now he had endeavoured to make sure that all on board reached port alive by tying up the troublemakers. The only one that he had attempted to kill, and that in order to save his own life, was John Howes. Now his reasoning changed. He judged that the sailors, whose plot he had been so successful in confounding, were guilty of a plan of mutiny — as their abandonment by Providence, in the form of the two ships that failed to rescue them, would seem to indicate — and so according to the law of all maritime nations, they deserved the death sentence. Their being abandoned by Heaven was, he believed, a further indication that God had designed them for this punishment. If God had not wanted them punished by death, then he would have ensured that one of the two passing ships rescued them. The fact that God had not caused them to be rescued was proof of their guilt. Having convinced himself of the justice of killing his men, Captain Stewart steeled himself against any feelings of mercy that might interfere with his plan, by convincing himself that in addition to being just, the killing of his men was necessary.

Standing on the quarterdeck, and watching the stern of the strange boat diminishing as it sailed towards the horizon, he flung aside his pistols, which he had found almost useless as weapons. He picked up a crowbar, which he had used earlier in the voyage as an implement of self-defence. Then he called on the boys to follow him, and rushed below. The men received no warning of their fate until the captain entered the cabin exclaiming in ominous and emphatic tones: 'The curse of God is upon you all.'

Little Hammond on his day bed saw the crowbar and the expression on Captain Stewart's face, and guessed his intentions. He jumped up from his bed, and entreated the captain not to take the crowbar to the helpless, bound men.

The captain ignored the boy, and then began, with ruthless energy, the dreadful work of death. The captain started with the second mate, William Swanson, smashing the crowbar down heavily on his head, and shouting, 'Ye ruffians, you intended to kill me; I will now take your lives!'

Blood and brains spattered in all directions, and Hammond's clothes were soon wet through, but the captain took no notice.

Blood ran across the deck of the cabin, and poured into the lazarette where the first mate, William Smith, lay throbbing with pain, in awful suspense, wondering when his turn would come. Blow by blow Captain Stewart made his way around the cabin, killing the ostler James Morley next, then the carpenter John Cramer, the seaman Francis Sullivan, his crewmate John Keating and the ostler Timothy Connell. Young Hammond, followed behind him, pleading with the captain to spare the innocent men. 'At least, spare some of them to take the ship home,' he begged in desperation. But to no avail.

His seventh and last victim was Captain Raynes. Aware of his inevitable fate, Raynes was praying fervently when Captain Stewart approached. He paused for a moment and said, 'James, I put a heavy curse on you, but now I take it off.' Then the fatal blow fell on James Raynes' head, and he lost consciousness.

Stewart continued to address his men as 'Ye ruffians'. His hoarse muttering sounded like the growling of an animal to the terror-stricken boys. He had now dealt mortal blows to six of the men, but still they groaned in agony as life slipped from their bodies. Stewart, suddenly unsure that his task had been successfully completed, seized the carpenter's axe that had fallen from the boy Richard's hands. With deliberate and determined blows he once again struck each of his seven victims on the head. Panting now from his exertions, the captain swapped the axe for the crowbar, and struck it through the air hole that had been made in the deck above Smith's prison in the lazarette. The pointed end of the crowbar glanced the side of Smith's head, and penetrated the collar of his shirt. Captain Stewart judged from the resistance to his blow that he must have made a direct hit, but he was not satisfied that he had killed the mate. He took up a sharper instrument, the long-handled harpoon that Deaves had let fall, to finish the job. He repeatedly plunged this instrument with all his might through the air hole in the direction where his prisoner lay. Smith received a series of cuts to his head, ears and side, then let out a howl as one of his eyes was struck with a direct hit.

The captain, still doubtful that his attack had been wholly successful, took up the axe again, and broke up a portion of the cabin deck in order to get a better aim at his victim. Then he repeated his stabs with the harpoon. Smith in his desperation had managed to roll his body slightly to one side, so that the new rain of blows from the lethal point of the sharp weapon glanced past his body, and struck into the mass of hides on which he was lying, giving Captain Stewart the impression that he had scored several direct hits such as no man could survive. 'He is dead, for good,' he said to the boys. And so the work of death was finished.

9

A Meeting in the Forepeak

When Captain Stewart had finished (as he thought) dealing with the chief mate, the last man he had to kill, his spirits rose. He later told William Scoresby that he felt 'as if released from an intolerable anxiety'. He became unnaturally animated and excited, feeling deeply satisfied with his day's work. This quickly turned to a sense of triumph, and suddenly his appetite, which had been non-existent for days, returned in full force. He ordered the boys to bring him some of the meat that he had been given by the captain of the *Mary Harriet*, and some strong spirits and water. The boys ran to obey his orders, amazed that anyone could think of eating amid the scene of bloody carnage, with the stench of death already permeating the air.

Captain Stewart sat in his usual chair in the cabin, apparently oblivious to the blood and gore around him, and looked at his plate of beef with satisfaction. Before he drank, he held up his glass, and pointed out to the awestruck boys that his hand was as steady as it had been before the deed was done. 'See, boys, how firm my hand is, as if I had not killed them! I could walk over them like dead dogs,' he said, before raising his glass to his lips and drinking deeply. Then he ate his meal with great pleasure, and drained his glass of rum and water.

The four young boys looked on, silenced by the captain's behaviour in the presence of seven dead men, men who less than an hour ago had been as much alive as they were now. For Hammond, this disrespectful behaviour, so untypical of the Captain Stewart he knew of old, confirmed what he had known for so long: the captain was stark, staring mad.

The captain, sitting in his usual chair, talked away to the boys as if this were just another normal day at sea, not the day on which seven of their shipmates lay around them, brutally slain. Captain Stewart congratulated Deaves, Scully and Richards on the manly part they had taken in the brave adventure, and assured them once again that they would each receive a reward of at least a hundred guineas. Richards would get £2,000 for saving his life with his axe. He himself, the captain continued, would get £7,000 or £8,000 from Lloyds, and the biggest ship out of London.

Night was now beginning to fall, and as

darkness approached Captain Stewart began to think about the risk of being set upon by the one member of his crew whom he believed was still alive: John Howes. He made preparations to ensure his own safety during the night that lay ahead. First he lashed the skylight of the main cabin firmly shut. Then he barricaded the companionway leading down to the cabin by nailing a transverse bar across it, and further securing it with staples. As an extra warning, he suspended a speaking trumpet in the passageway between the companionway and the cabin in such a way that it would rattle loudly if an intruder managed to get past the barricades. With the main cabin thus fortified, he sent the boys, including young Hammond, whose normal resting place was saturated with blood, to rest in an inner cabin, and he himself retired to sleep in another of the compartments opening into the main cabin, the chamber of the dead. At last Captain Stewart had fulfilled his great yearning to be rid of his 'mutinous' crew, and was able to sleep soundly.

★ ★ ★

Hidden away in the forepeak of the ship, the seaman John Howes lay in the refuge he had reached by crawling along the top of the cargo of hogsheads of Barbados sugar. On first reaching his resting place, he had bound up his bleeding head with the kerchief that he wore around his neck. He lay for some hours, drifting in and out of consciousness. His suffering had started with being trussed up hand and foot before spending the most uncomfortable night of his long seafaring life, and culminated, after being shot at five times, in a life-and-death struggle with his commander and his three juvenile henchmen. Howes winced at the memory of the young boys, carrying weapons so large they could hardly lift them, in thrall to their captain and commander, forced to back him up in his murderous intentions. Then he flinched with pain: his head throbbed intolerably, his hand throbbed, too, to a different beat, and his side was stinging and still oozing blood. But worst of all was an excruciating thirst that soon became too much to bear. Never in his long life had he been so dry. Whatever the consequences, he had to have water. In spite of the risk of being seen by the captain or more likely, one of the boys, he gathered together his little remaining strength, and crept back across the hogsheads and up on deck. He was relieved to see that it was dusk, and was reassured by the apparent lack of activity. The wheel was lashed, the ship

112

hove-to under low sail, the breeze light and steady. Apart from the gentle lapping of the water against the hull, there was no sound to be heard on board, not a murmur. The ship lay under a solemn repose, like the silence you would hear in church: a hush unlike any hush he had ever heard before aboard ship. The overcast sky, with neither star nor moon, added to the eeriness. Perhaps, he thought, his companions had somehow managed to fall asleep; perhaps they had been released and gone away while he had lain hidden, struggling to stay awake. Howes was not sure how much time had passed, nor what goings-on he might have missed while suffering his own agony, alone in the forepeak. He crawled slowly and silently across the deck to the water cask, only to find it empty. He listened carefully for any sound of life, and hearing none, he pulled himself upright, wincing again at the new sources of pain that emerged with his new position, and anxiously continued to search the deck and then the fo'c'sle for a drop of precious water. At last he found some, and slaked his thirst. He also found the carpenter's axe that Richards had used on his head, and one of the captain's pistols, lost in their recent struggle. He put these, his water supply and a few coconuts that were lying about on deck

113

into a sack, which he dragged along with him, across the hogsheads and back into the forepeak. Then he spent sometime rearranging the casks so that he occupied a hidden space, fortified against any intrusion. He took another drink of water, then put his head down on the sack, and rested undisturbed all night.

* ★ ★

Meanwhile, under the floor of the main cabin, Chief Mate William Smith, now minus one eye and most of an ear, wounded in the side and saturated with the blood of his shipmates, lay as still as possible in his tomb-like lazarette. Assuming Smith was dead, and not wanting to step accidentally in the hole through which he had attacked him with the harpoon and trip himself up, the captain had nailed a piece of board over the opening before settling down to his meal. Smith listened in horror as the captain, having ordered a large meal, boasted to the boys of the steadiness of his hand, before tucking into a plate of beef washed down by grog. The captain's seat was almost immediately above the lazarette, so that his feet rested on it, inches from Smith's head, while he enjoyed his fine meal.

Then to talk of money matters and savour a glass of grog, when the good men of the crew lay freshly slaughtered all around! Smith had thought he'd seen and heard it all in his years at sea, but this was the limit of abomination: yet he had thought the captain such a kind man, and knew him to be devout. It was the dream that started it all, the dream that turned the captain superstitious, Smith remembered, thinking back to the early days of the voyage, which now seemed like another life, a heavenly other life . . .

Smith waited until he heard the captain move from his seat, and listened as he barricaded himself and the boys into the great cabin. He heard the captain send the boys off to an inner cabin; then the captain's footsteps ceased as he too went to take some rest. Smith waited another while to make sure Captain Stewart had settled, before making a desperate effort to release himself from his bonds. No longer afraid of being overheard, he struggled harder than ever before, and managed to stretch one of his hands far enough to reach his pocket knife; with the knife he was able to cut the lashings on his hands, and then free his legs.

The lazarette led into the cargo hold, and a narrow space had been left between the hogsheads of sugar and the beams above, so

115

that Smith, like Howes, was able to crawl away on his belly from the scene of slaughter. Like Howes, he headed for the front of the hold, as being the most likely hiding place in the ship. Howes, hearing movement in the darkness of the hold, asked in a whisper who was there. Smith immediately recognised the voice of the missing crew member, and the two shipmates were reunited, hacked and maimed, still suffering severely but alive, and now in company. Howes gave an account of his near-fatal encounter with Captain Stewart and the boys. Then Smith told Howes, as he had heard it, of the slaughter of their seven comrades by crowbar and axe, the river of blood, and his own narrow escape. Howes shuddered with dismay when he heard Smith's words, his body trembling from head to toe with a weakness such as he had never felt before. He closed his eyes in horror at his shipmates' fate, and prayed to God for the repose of their souls:

William Swanson
James Morley
John Cramer
Francis Sullivan
John Keating
Timothy Connell
Captain James Goold Raynes

10

Rescue

Captain Stewart did not sleep as well as he would have liked. His mind was agitated, and he woke suddenly at the slightest provocation, before falling back into an uneasy unconsciousness. Daylight had not yet broken when he was woken abruptly again. He sprang up from his berth and looked out of the cabin's windows, where he could clearly see that the brig was under way. She was going fast through the water, and from the position of her head by the cabin compass she was on a course very nearly in the direction of Cape Clear, their Irish landfall. The Captain immediately concluded that John Howes must have survived his multiple wounds, and taken the helm. As he tore away the barricades he had put up last night, he shouted up to the quarterdeck 'John, keep her a point more to leeward!' But there was no answer. The helm was lashed as he had left it. The apparent headway of the vessel was an illusion, merely the accidental effect of a gust of wind in the sails.

Going back below, Captain Stewart noticed that his watch, which had stopped ticking some weeks previously, and been left hanging beside his berth, was now going again. The boys must have been meddling with it while he slept. From this he concluded that the boys were not as passive and subdued as they seemed. They were not to be trusted. If they could meddle with his watch while he slept, what else might they do? This was proof of their evil intentions towards him. They would have to be disarmed and tied up.

The boys had been woken at 4 a.m. by the captain calling out to Howes on the wheel, and had shadowed him as he went on deck, wondering if Howes could have recovered so quickly, and if he had, why he was showing himself and taking the wheel. But there was no one at the wheel, and the ship was still not going anywhere. They went back down below, and reported the incident to young Hammond.

The apprentices were taken by surprise when Captain Stewart called them over and ordered them to surrender their arms. John Deaves brought his harpoon and laid it at his captain's feet. Daniel Scully followed with his granes, and Henry Richards gave up the axe with which he had replaced the one lost in the struggle with Howes. Next he ordered the boys to hold out their hands in front of them to be tied. This alarmed them greatly, and they backed away as one, pleading with him not to tie them up. They had seen what had happened to the men who let themselves be tied, and were frightened that a similar fate awaited them. Thomas Hammond pleaded earnestly and anxiously for the boys to be left at liberty. He reminded the captain of their obedience, and the essential help that they could give the captain in sailing the ship, and respectfully reminded the captain in his solemn way that the boys were not guilty of any crime, nor had they disobeyed any order, and that it would not be fair to do them any harm.

The word 'harm' had an immediate effect on Captain Stewart. Suddenly he became the man that the boys had known in the earlier stages of the voyage, a gentle, kind man. He denied with obvious sincerity having any intention of doing the boys any harm. He assured them that they would be perfectly safe tied up, and swore an oath on the Bible to that effect.

He was leaving young Hammond at liberty, he explained, because he knew him to be an innocent child. And in case they still had any doubts of the sincerity of his declarations, he put a loaded pistol into Thomas Hammond's quaking hands, giving the young boy authority to shoot him dead if he should attempt to hurt his youthful comrades. Hammond trembled as he held the pistol, for he knew that once the boys were tied, he would be the only one at liberty on the ship, and at the mercy of a dangerous madman.

Captain Stewart started with the senior apprentice, John Deaves, tying up his hands, then ordering him to sit on the cabin deck, while he tied up his feet. Then he tied Daniel Scully in the same way, and finally Henry Richards. Hardly had he finished his task, when they heard a voice hailing the ship. The four boys and Captain Stewart were each overwhelmed with relief at the sound. The voice called again, and Captain Stewart, who had been reviving himself with a pinch of snuff, stuck his head and shoulders out of the cabin window, still waving the bottle of snuff in the air in his excitement. He saw a ship hove-to alongside, and a stranger waving at him from the deck. 'For God Almighty's sake come to my assistance,' he shouted.

'What's the matter?' shouted the stranger.

'There's been a mutiny on board. I killed eight of the men, but one made his escape.'

Then he repeated his entreaties for assistance, adding, in his anxiety at the way that the two previous boats had abandoned him, that if it was refused, he would jump overboard. He was followed on deck by young Hammond, who had immediately recognised the ship that was coming to their aid, and tried to tell his frantic captain that the boat approaching was known to them.

Stewart, too impatient to listen to the little boy, rushed up on deck, and jumped up on the taffrail, as if to fulfill his threat. The captain of the strange boat had long ago identified the *Mary Russell*. For the ship that had come to their rescue was the *Mary Stubbs* of Campobello, New Brunswick, under the command of Captain Robert Callendar, the very brig to which the *Mary Russell* had been rafted in Barbados.

'Hold on there, Stewart, I'm coming to help,' Callendar shouted. His men were already lowering the boat.

★ ★ ★

The *Mary Stubbs* had left Barbados on 10 May, one day after the *Mary Russell*, bound for Belfast, and had followed a similar course thus far. At about 8 a.m. on Monday 23 June, the steward of the *Mary Stubbs* spotted a brig at no great distance, lying to, and pointed it out to his captain. Callendar reckoned they were then about 300 miles off the south coast of Ireland, and was puzzled to see a vessel lying to. He guessed that perhaps they had mistaken their position, and were trying for soundings, but this would have been most unusual, as they were still so far from land. As they got nearer the brig, this explanation was abandoned, for at closer quarters the crew of the *Mary Stubbs* could see that the ship had an ensign halfway up the mast, flying upside down, the recognised signal of distress. Captain Callendar changed course to head straight for the distressed vessel, which was shortly identified as the *Mary Russell*. When he got close, seeing nobody on deck, he hailed her repeatedly through his speaking trumpet. He sailed all the way around her, still seeing nobody on deck; then he came alongside, and finally crossed her stern, which is when his call was answered from inside the cabin.

When young Hammond finally got his attention, and explained that their rescuers were known to them, Captain Stewart was overjoyed to recognise the amiable American. As the boat rowed across from one brig to the other, he shouted encouragement at the men in it. 'Don't be afraid to come on board. All the mutineers are dead, but one.'

The first person to reach the deck of the brig was Captain Callendar, and the two men greeted each other warmly. Callendar remembered that, ironically, he had leant Captain Stewart his spare ensign, which now hung upside down from the mast, shortly before the *Mary Russell* had sailed. As he and the captain greeted each other, Hammond ran below to start untying the boys.

Stewart handed Callendar the pistol that Hammond had left on the deck, then taking him aft to the quarterdeck, he stamped his foot through the cabin skylight, and showed the American skipper the bodies of his crew, still lying where they had been slain. Callendar was shocked into silence by the carnage below, the terribly wounded men and the bloodied floor. And there in the midst of it all were young Hammond and the ship's three boys, untying each other.

Captain Stewart led his silent visitor down into the cabin, delighted that at last he had a witness to his handiwork. Callendar recognised among the dead Captain Raynes. Then, through the dried gore, he identified the sailors who had been familiar figures aboard the brig during their time in Barbados: the second mate, William Swanson, the carpenter John Cramer, the two seamen Francis Sullivan and John Keating. He recognised too the lads who had come over with the mules, Timothy Connell and John Morley. All dead, tied hand and foot, then trussed up again neck to ankle, and bludgeoned most horribly about the head. Callendar had never seen such carnage. Stewart seemed immensely pleased with himself, strutting up and down with a self-satisfied expression on his face, talking in a boastful tone, apparently exulting in his achievement. Callendar just caught the end of his sentence 'I could trample over them like a parcel of dead sheep.' Stewart puffed out his chest, and turned to Callendar smiling: 'Was I not a valiant little fellow, to kill so many men?'

Callendar was shocked to the core. Then Stewart added, 'If only Howes were dead too, I'd be satisfied.'

'What happened, Stewart?' Callendar asked urgently. 'Tell me the details.'

Then Callendar heard the story of how Captain Raynes and the seaman John Howes had raised a mutiny on board, and were going to take the vessel from him. To discourage them he had been obliged to break his navigation instruments and throw his charts overboard. He had taken various other measures to make sure they did not succeed in their plan to murder him. As proof of their wicked intentions he assured the visiting captain that he had a paper in his prayer book, which was in his chest pocket, signed by the three ship's boys, stating that they had all witnessed a mutiny on board. Stewart added: 'I've been so dreadfully troubled by fear of murder, I haven't slept for twenty-seven days and nights!' He pleaded urgently with Callendar to protect him, and take him home safely to his wife and family. Callendar promised Stewart he would do so, and Stewart seemed to calm down a little.

He asked Callendar to help him search the ship for the missing seaman, the leader of the mutineers, John Howes. Armed only with the small pistol that Stewart had put into his hand when he boarded, Callendar was wary of pursuing the mutineer. He had no reason to doubt the facts of the case as stated by his peer, Captain Stewart, and he reckoned that Howes, having failed at his attempt to mutiny, would fight back with the abandon of an already condemned man. But he overcame his reluctance, and he and the sailors who had rowed him over, helped by the ship's boys, who said they had seen Howes' legs hanging out below, began to search the ship.

The boys found Howes by the simple ruse of following the trail of blood that lead from the fo'c'sle to the forepeak. They guided Captain Stewart to the wounded seaman, who was lying in his hiding place. He had covered himself in a large bag, and the expression of his features was almost obliterated by a mask of dried blood. Howes was in a poor state, and at the sight of his captain his low spirits sank even further. This was the end: he had no fight left in him. Then he caught sight of a stranger, looking over the shoulder of his would-be murderer, and called out: 'Is that you, Captain Callendar?'

'It is. Get up and come along with me.'

'Willingly, sir, if you will protect me from Captain Stewart, I'll come on the fo'c'sle.' Before he left the hold, he called out to his companion, the chief mate, William Smith. Smith appeared from the shadows behind Howes, covered only by an old shirt. One of his eyes was hanging from its socket, there was a gash down his cheek, and one of his ears was missing. He was covered in stab wounds. The shirt was stuck to one side of his body by dried blood. He winced in pain at every step.

At the sight of Smith, Captain Stewart started back in amazement: 'I thought you were dead!' he said. Then he paused for a moment, reflecting on the extraordinary fact of Smith's escape from death, and said: 'I now believe you were innocent. I am sorry for having hurt you. It was God spared your life.'

Stewart appealed urgently to Smith to confirm what he had told Captain Callendar:

126

that the men he had killed had, within Smith's hearing, confessed to mutiny. Smith mumbled what sounded like an agreement.

The sight of Howes had put Stewart into a state of high anxiety. He could not stay on the same boat as Howes, as he was convinced that Howes would renew his murderous attack, in retribution for the wounds Stewart had inflicted. Callendar thought the notion highly unlikely, but persuaded Howes to submit to a very slight lashing on his hands, simply to calm his captain's apprehensions.

Arrangements were now made to get the brig under way. Callendar offered to leave three of his men on board to help Stewart to sail her. He also agreed to remove the two wounded men, Smith and Howes, to his own vessel, for the sake of Captain Stewart's peace of mind. He also took the passenger, Master Hammond, with him. The boy was a pitiful sight, his suit of clothes saturated with blood, his pale face streaked with dried gore. As soon as they were on board the *Mary Stubbs*, Callendar ordered hot coffee for the exhausted lad. Then he told one of his ship's boys to fetch his spare clothes, which he gave to Hammond. Both brigs set sail in company for Cork at 11 a.m. on Monday 23 June 1828. Thomas Hammond welcomed the familiar motion of a ship under way, heading home, before he fell asleep in a clean, dry berth under a clean, dry blanket.

The two brigs sailed on towards the Irish coast, taking full advantage of the brisk breeze. Captain Stewart gave orders about the course and the trimming of the sails to Captain Callendar's men. The wind freshened to such an extent that Captain Callendar was unable to board the *Mary Russell* again until 8 a.m. on Wednesday. They were now about 15 miles westsouthwest of Cape Clear, Ireland's most southerly point. Captain Stewart was pacing the deck of the *Mary Russell*, and seemed deeply preoccupied.

'How are you, Stewart?' Callendar asked.

'I'm not very well,' was the answer. The pale-faced Stewart looked warily behind him at the sailor from the *Mary Stubbs* who was at the helm, and the two other men standing near him, and beckoned Callendar to come closer. Then he confided in a fretful whisper that he feared the men from the *Mary Stubbs* were going to murder him. They were plotting together to kill him in revenge for his punishment of the mutineers. This confirmed Callendar's suspicions, which had been kindled by hearing their version of events from Smith and Howes. Stewart was deranged: it was now obvious, with Stewart once more voicing unjustified suspicions, permanently fearing for his safety for no reason. His eyes had an abnormally bright glint, and his skin showed an unnatural pallor for a sailor returning from Barbados.

Callendar tried to reassure Stewart, by saying jokingly that he hadn't put two of his best seamen on board in order to injure him: they were there to sail the brig. Then Callendar was briefly distracted by something he spotted up forward, which he went to rectify. As he was doing so, he heard a shout of 'Lord help me!' and looking back saw Stewart standing on the main chain, then launching himself into the air and jumping overboard.

The boat which had carried Captain Callendar across was towing astern, and he ordered his men to pick Stewart up. Stewart was a strong swimmer, and had no trouble staying afloat. He was picked up, and brought back on board. Captain Callendar had strong words for his fellow captain, rebuking him for his reckless conduct, which had put his life in danger. Stewart, dripping wet, head bowed, seemed suitably chastened by his folly. Callendar left him to get changed, and went to the fo'c'sle to look out for land. It was an overcast day with a low sky and poor visibility. But the captain could smell land ahead, and knew they were not far off.

Hardly had he turned his back than Stewart had taken advantage of his absence to jump overboard once more. Once more he was rescued promptly by the boat, and brought back on board. To prevent any more attempts at self-destruction, Captain Callendar ordered Stewart's legs to be tied. The two sailors from the *Mary Stubbs* were reluctant to continue sailing the *Mary Russell* with such a dangerous character on board, a man who seemed as ready to sacrifice his own life as he had been to take the lives of others. Captain Callendar reckoned the best solution was to relieve his men of the source of their concern by taking Stewart on board his own vessel for the remainder of the return journey. Once they were aboard, both vessels set sail again for the port of Cove, both with lookouts at their stem for they were now sailing through patches of fog.

Once safely aboard the *Mary Stubbs*, Captain Stewart, who had been untied to make the crossing, agreed to take some coffee, and was then persuaded to rest his weary body. Callendar hoped that rest would soothe Stewart's agitated feelings. But Stewart was too worked up to rest for more than a few minutes. Up he went on deck again, but there he saw a sight that induced a state of sheer panic: his two wounded sailors, Smith and Howes. Terrified that they would now take vengeance on him for trying to kill them, he went back down to the cabin to seek some weapon of defence. He came back brandishing a carving knife and fork. When Callendar objected to this, Stewart explained that unless he had the means of defending himself, his men would take his life. He was trembling badly, and seemed greatly afraid of the two men.

In order to pacify his colleague, Captain Callendar ordered Smith and Howes below. Out of Stewart's earshot he explained to them that he was locking them up temporarily for their own safety, and in the hope of calming Captain Stewart, who was suffering badly from his nerves. Back on deck, he reassured Stewart that the men were securely locked up, but still Stewart was afraid that they would get him somehow.

Suddenly the fog lifted, and both captains saw three hookers — small fishing sloops — not far off. Stewart begged Callendar to haul up to one of them, to confirm where the land lay. Callendar, who would have done this whether Stewart asked him to or not, was giving orders for the manoeuvre, and all on deck were occupied trimming sails. Captain Stewart saw his chance, and jumped overboard a third time. He could then be seen swimming strongly towards the nearest hooker. As the *Mary Stubbs* came within hailing distance of the hooker, Captain Callendar pointed out to the fishermen that there was a man overboard. The hooker immediately changed course, and picked up the swimmer. Meanwhile, the *Mary Stubbs* hove to, expecting to receive Captain Stewart back on board once more. But to the surprise of everyone, the hooker sailed away from them, heading west.

Pursuit was pointless, so Captain Callendar resumed his course for Cork Harbour, the *Mary Stubbs* sailing in company with the *Mary Russell* for the rest of the day and evening, arriving safely about 10 p.m., and dropping anchor off the Cove of Cork.

Part Two

The Inquest

11

William Scoresby on the *Mary Russell*

William Scoresby, his brother-in-law Colonel Fitzgerald and a third, unnamed friend were among the first visitors to the *Mary Russell* on Thursday 26 June 1828. The brig was already in charge of a civil officer, and he and two of the apprentice boys were the only people on board. As was the custom, the Coroner's inquest was scheduled to open in the presence of the deceased later the same day. Colonel Fitzgerald, as the first magistrate on the scene, examined the two boys aboard the *Mary Russell* at considerable length about the events leading to the killings. Then the visitors proceeded to the *Mary Stubbs*, which lay alongside, where they met the third apprentice, and the two other survivors, chief mate William Smith, and the seaman John Howes. There is no record of the Scoresby party talking to Thomas Hammond. Perhaps the child was briefly allowed home after his ordeal until the start of the inquest.

It is a lucky coincidence for posterity that one of the first people to board the *Mary*

Russell that morning was William Scoresby, who, as a retired whaling captain, a distinguished author, a scientific observer (elected Fellow of the Royal Society in 1824), and a minister of the church, was unusually well qualified to report and comment on what he found. Scoresby was a native of Whitby on the north Yorkshire coast, and the second generation of an accomplished seafaring family. His father, William Scoresby (1760–1829), was the first of his line to go to sea, becoming a successful whaling captain. He pioneered the North Sea whaling fishery, and is credited, among other achievements, with the invention of the crow's nest, a framework installed on the main top mast, its sides protected by leather or canvas, accessible through a trapdoor in its base, equipped with a telescope, flags, speaking trumpet and firearms, which made life much easier — and safer — for the lookouts scanning the sea for whales. In 1806 William Scoresby senior reached latitude 81° 30′ North, within 510 miles of the North Pole, the furthest north any ship had been.

His son William, who was born in 1789, first went to sea in 1800 at the tender age of eleven. He managed this by hiding his hat, and pretending he could not find it on board, while saying goodbye to his father, so that the ship sailed with him. His father put him ashore on the Shetland Islands, but young William found a boat, and persuaded its owners to row him out to his father's ship again. In 1803, at the conventional age of fourteen, he became officially apprenticed to his father. He became a mate at seventeen, and at twenty-one, the minimum age for a ship's captain, was given his first command. While onshore in the winter months, outside the whaling season, he studied at Edinburgh University, where his main interest was science. Later in London he was introduced to Sir Joseph Banks, who had sailed on Captain Cook's first voyage in 1788, and was an important patron of scientific researchers. Both Banks and Scoresby's colleagues at Edinburgh University encouraged this remarkable young man's interests in scientific experiment, and in surveying the land, geology and fauna of the polar regions. He was the first person to observe snowflakes under the microscope in various weather conditions, and to make drawings of their unique hexagonal shapes.

In 1820 he published his book *An Account of the Arctic Regions*, which is described by the *Oxford Dictionary of National Biography* as 'the foundation stone of Arctic science'. (Darwin, writing from aboard the *Beagle* off Rio de la Plata in 1833, begged his sister to send 'Humphry Davy's *Consolations in Travel*,

137

alongside Hutton on geology, Scoresby on Arctic regions, and Paul Scrope on volcanoes'.) Scoresby wrote it while in Liverpool, supervising the building of a new ship, the *Baffin*, which was being constructed to his own design for Arctic expeditions. The *Baffin* was launched in February 1820 and Scoresby was given command. In 1822 during his second voyage on the *Baffin* he mapped the east coast of Greenland. On returning from this trip he was informed of the death of his beloved wife, with whom he had two sons, and who shared his intense interest in religion. In 1823, after twenty annual voyages (during which time he only spent one summer in England), he decided to retire from the sea and join the church. His scientific colleagues disapproved, regretting the loss of his lively mind to scientific pursuits. His friends included Sir Humphry Davy, Sir Walter Scott and his fellow-explorer Baron Humboldt.

Scoresby was ordained at York in July 1825, and was appointed curate at Bessingley near Bridlington. He went from being a wealthy sea captain, earning around £800 a year to a curate's stipend of £40. In May 1827 he was appointed rector of the Mariner's Church in Liverpool, also known as the Floating Church. This was located in a former warship, capable of accommodating about a

138

thousand persons, largely seafaring men. As a preacher he became known for his use of nautical metaphors; he had changed, he said, from being a fisher of whales to a fisher of men.

William Scoresby was in Cove in June 1828 because he had celebrated his marriage to Miss Elizabeth Fitzgerald on 11 May. Scoresby had been fascinated by Ireland since a visit to the Giant's Causeway in 1819, and returned several times. Now he had found himself an Irish wife. Miss Fitzgerald was the eldest daughter of the late Colonel R. Uniacke Penrose Fitzgerald, a pillar of Cork's Protestant community, and the owner of Corkbegg, a large estate of prime agricultural land on the eastern flank of Cork Harbour.

In 1835 Scoresby published *Memorials of the Sea*, a book that combines memoirs of his days as a sea captain and explorer with religious reflections. Books of sermons were greatly in vogue at the time, and this one had the bonus of exciting seafaring yarns. One of the most compelling sections of the book is a 167-page narrative simply entitled 'The *Mary Russell*'. Here Scoresby gives a meticulous and detailed account of the events of the voyage, as told to him first-hand by the survivors, supplemented by contemporary court reporting. He also tells of his subsequent friendship with Captain Stewart, and reflects on the moral lessons to be learnt from 'the tragical proceedings'.

Scoresby and his brother-in-law, the magistrate Colonel Fitzgerald, found that, apart from the civil officer, there were only two apprentice boys on board the *Mary Russell*. As soon as the visitors reached the deck, the boys led them to the open hatch of the cabin's skylight, where they had an unobstructed view of what Scoresby calls ' the sickening scene beneath'. He continues:

Five swollen bodies, lashed on their backs, mangled with ghastly wounds, and clotted with gore, were lying conspicuously visible beneath [the skylight] with the lower extremities of two others seen projecting from the mate's cabin; the whole of which had remained, I believe, undisturbed, from the hour of the massacre. The body of the unhappy Raynes, with the head and face shockingly mangled, lay almost immediately beneath the skylight — a frightful object; and the rest, in various degrees of conspicuousness, combined in the completion of the appalling spectacle.

The veteran of twenty voyages to the Arctic, witness to the slaying of innumerable whales with all the attendant blood and gore, reported that the scene he contemplated in Cork Harbour made such a deep impression on his mind that he still recalled it vividly many years later. He honestly admitted that 'It required more than an ordinary nerve and habit of self-possession to contemplate unsickened the dreadful charnel house'.

Colonel Fitzgerald questioned the two boys at considerable length about the events leading to the carnage. The two men then went aboard the *Mary Stubbs* which, just as in Barbados, was alongside the *Mary Russell*. Here they met the third apprentice (who is unnamed by Scoresby, but seems to be Daniel Scully), chief mate Smith and seaman Howes. The latter pair of survivors were seen in a religious sense by Reverend Scoresby as 'monuments of God's preserving Mercy', and excited his intense interest. He describes both men as shockingly mutilated, even though they were able to come on deck. Their wounds had not yet been attended to, and these, and the state of their torn and bloodstained clothing, spoke eloquently of the terrible experience they had recently been through, showing how close they had come to being slaughtered. Smith talked freely about the details of the day when his shipmates were killed, but Howes spoke more cautiously, as if wary of the danger of incriminating himself. But he was praised for answering Scoresby's questions clearly and to the point. Scoresby judged Howes to be an unusually courageous and intelligent man of great willpower and tenacity, with a clear idea of right and wrong. Just to see the brave, badly wounded sailor leaning against the bulwark of the vessel as he talked conjured up in Scoresby's mind a vivid picture of the terrible scenes in which Howes had recently been a player. Scoresby immediately recognised in Howes a man of outstanding probity:

His face was considerably weather-beaten, and his countenance, as it appeared to me, was strongly marked, combining with some severity of expression an indication of straight forward manliness of character. He was the very man one would have picked out of a whole ship's company as likely to be the foremost in any act of daring . . . He seemed the very character whom one could believe capable of saying to his determined commander, when standing over him armed with deadly weapons, 'I will die before I will again submit to being tied!'

The mate Smith did not seem to Scoresby to be in the same league of heroism, but nevertheless, the sight of him aroused great sympathy:

> The tremendous violence attempted against him had left very impressive marks. His wounded eye, and cheek and head not only bore testimony to the truthfulness of his account of his own adventures, but evinced likewise, as an unquestionable fact, this measure of his peril, that there had been but a hair's breadth betwixt him and death.

As soon as the news reached the offices of Cork city's leading newspaper, the *Constitution*, they dispatched a gentleman 'by Express', who arrived a few hours before the Coroner and his party. The scene with which he opens his report marks the start of the frenzy of curiosity about the case and its villain, Captain Stewart, that was to grip Cork city for the next six weeks:

> This City was thrown into a state of confusion and disarray on Thursday, by the arrival of the ship *Mary Stubbs*, bound from Barbados to Belfast, and who arrived that morning at Cove, bringing with her the *Mary Russell*, which she found in a distressful state at sea, with seven persons including passengers and crew dead in their Cabin. And

their bodies in a most mangled state, and two men most severely wounded. This unparalleled and afflicting occurrence was perpetuated by the Captain, who shortly after the *Mary Stubbs* bore down jumped into the sea, and was picked up by a fishing boat belonging to Berehaven. The only persons that escaped the vengeance of this demon were three boys belonging to the ship, and a mere child a passenger!

While Scoresby describes the view of the corpses through the skylight, the reporter from the *Constitution*, who arrived after Scoresby's party but well in advance of the officials who were to open the inquest, describes in detail the scene that confronted him on entering the cabin. Both men mentioned the physical effort that it took to confront the scene of decomposition without succumbing to nausea. The date of the inquest was Thursday 26 June, and the bodies had lain in the cabin since the previous Sunday (22 June), in increasingly warm weather. The *Constitution* warns readers that the description that follows is 'appalling in the extreme':

There were seven human beings with their skulls so battered, that scarcely a vestige of them was left for recognition, with a frightful mass of coagulated blood — all strewed about the cabin, and nearly a hundred weight of cords binding down their bodies to strong iron bolts, which had been driven into the floor for that murderous purpose. Some of the bodies were bound round in six places, with several coils of rope around their necks — and all were in a state of decomposition so that it required a constitution of no ordinary strength to bear up against the spectacle and the effluvia, that arose from a confined cabin.

At about three o'clock the city sheriffs, the Senior Coroner (Henry Hardy, Esq.), Dr Sharpe and several gentlemen arrived from Cork city. The bodies were then raised by a block and tackle to be examined by the surgeon. The *Constitution's* reporter at this point thankfully spares us the details: 'We will make no attempt to describe further their state — suffice to say that it was sufficient to appall the stoutest hearts, and to show man off in his own insignificance, and to strike him with astonishment at the inscrutable will of PROVIDENCE.'

When the surgeon had finished his examination, the jury was sworn in. The names of these twelve respectable men were: John B. Cotter, John Jackson, Edmond Burke, John Barry, Daniel Callaghan, Daniel Buckley, Michael Walsh, Michael Hennessy, Daniel Casey, James Enright, W. L. Perrier and Charles Robinson. They were addressed briefly by the Coroner, Henry Hardy. He referred emotionally to the tragic event, and informed the jury that it was their duty to ascertain how Captain James Raynes, Francis Sullivan, John Keating, James Morley, Timothy Connell, John Cramer and William Swanson came by their deaths. The *Freeman's Journal*, which carried its report in the following week on 2 July, mentions that it was part of the jury's duty to inspect the corpses:

. . . the bodies . . . when inspected by the Jury, were lying on board the *Mary Russell*; they were all stretched along the floor of the cabin, and presented one of the most horrifying and dreadful sights that can well be imagined. The faces of all were lacerated in the most shocking manner, and they gave unquestionable evidence that the work of death had been executed with no ordinary degree of violence. It appeared also that the deceased had been fastened down with ropes to the floor, so as if attacked in that situation, to be incapable of making any resistance.

After this, the jury went on to examine the ship itself, and then began the examination of witnesses by hearing the evidence of Captain Robert Callendar of St Andrews, New Brunswick in North America, Master of the schooner *Mary Stubbs* of Campobello, New Brunswick. Captain Callendar was sworn in, and told the court that he had left Barbados aboard the *Mary Stubbs* on 10 May, bound for Belfast, the day after the *Mary Russell* had sailed for Cork. He had known Captain Stewart while they were in Barbados. Last Monday morning he came across the brig about 300 miles off the coast of Ireland, flying the distress signal. He hailed her three times, but got no answer. Neither did he see any person on deck until Captain Stewart put his head out of one of the windows with a bottle in his hand, which Callendar afterwards found contained snuff. He recounted going on board, and quoted Stewart's words 'For God Almighty's sake, come to my assistance!', and his saying that there was a mutiny on his vessel, and that he had killed eight men. At the end of his deposition, according to the *Constitution's* reporter, Callendar said 'he is of opinion that Captain Stewart was deranged, that his looks and appearance were quite different from what they were in the West Indies.'

Thomas Sharpe, Esq., Surgeon, was then sworn in. He reported on his inspection of the bodies of seven persons lying dead on board the brig, *Mary Russell* of Cork, and named the seven. He said that all the deceased were lying in the main cabin of the *Mary Russell*, and every one of them had extensive fractures of the skull:

James Raynes had a mortal fracture on the anterior part of the skull and face. William Swanson, a mortal fracture on the right side of his head. James Morley a mortal fracture on the right side and the back part of the head. Francis Sullivan's head on the left side was extensively fractured. John Cramer had the anterior part of his skull beaten in. Timothy Connell had a mortal fracture on the left side of his head, and John Keating's head on the left side and anterior part was mortally fractured and beaten in, all which fractures must have been occasioned by some very weighty pointed instrument, a crow bar, as deponent had been informed, and must have produced

148

almost instantaneous death. All said men were strongly tied by arms, legs and thighs, and partly by the neck, and were lying on what appeared to be mattresses.

At this point, it became apparent that there would not be enough time that day to complete hearing the depositions of the witnesses, and it was agreed to adjourn until the next day, and to resume the inquest in the Bridewell in Cork city.

Once the inquest had completed its initial stage aboard the *Mary Russell*, and adjourned until the next day, the Coroner Henry Hardy had coffins taken on board so that the remains of the deceased could be delivered to their respective families. Six of the deceased had left wives and families. We could find no death notices in the papers for the six humble seafarers, nor for the seventh victim, Captain Raynes, and no reports of the funerals. The only grave that has been located is that of Timothy Connell, in Kilmurry Graveyard, Passage West. It reads:

This stone was Erected
By PATRICK CONNELL in
memory of his Brother
TIMOTHY CONNELL who was

149

murdered on board of the
MARY RUSSELL 22nd June 1828
also as a burial place for himself
and Family

You gentle reader that do pass this way
attend a while adhere to what I say
By murder vile was I bereft of life
and parted from two lovely babes and wife
by CAPTAIN STEWART I met an early doom
on board the MARY RUSSELL the 22nd of June
Forced from this world to meet my GOD on high
with whom I hope to reign eternally. Amen

Aged 28 years

12

The Inquest Concluded

The second day of the inquest opened with the reading of two letters. These contained sensational news: Captain Stewart was alive and in custody in Skibbereen, and had confessed to the killing of his crew. But he had also accused them of mutiny, a serious crime, punishable by death.

The first letter had been written at 7 a.m. that same morning, and was from John Galway, Local Inspector, County Cork Constabulary, Ballincollig (on the western approach to Cork), to the Mayor of Cork. It enclosed a letter from Chief Constable Brownrigg, superintendent of the Constabulary in Carbery West, East Division (which included Skibbereen). It recounts how Captain Stewart had been given up by the coastguard to the Constable Station at Baltimore, the nearest port to Skibbereen. Stewart had confessed to killing seven of his crew, and wounding two, all of whom he alleged had mutinied. Stewart claimed that he had jumped overboard from the *Mary Russell* and swum to the *Mary Stubbs*. Still feeling that his life was in danger, he again jumped overboard from the *Mary Stubbs* and swam to a fishing boat, which picked him up and gave him in charge to the coastguard.

Brownrigg reports that Captain Stewart was well known in Skibbereen, and 'was always considered very humane; he is very respectably connected, being nephew to Dr Stewart of Clonakilty'. Dr Stewart was a clergyman, and a landholder at Kilgarriffe in Clonakilty, 32 km east of Skibbereen. The letter concludes:

At first I considered the statement a mere fabrication; but now I fear that it is but too true: and if he destroyed his unfortunate crew in the manner he says he did, it is one of the most horrible cases which has ever come before the public.

The above vessels having proceeded, as I understand, for Cork, I deem it proper to give you the earliest intelligence of the above lamentable circumstances; — and in order that you may apprise the authorities in Cork, of Wm. Stewart, the master of the *Mary Russell*, being in custody, about whose apprehension they are no doubt anxious.

The first witness, Daniel Scully, answered questions from the Coroner and the jury for over four hours. The boy is described as 'very intelligent', and became quite emotional when giving evidence, as did the jury. He told the Coroner's court that he was from Brickfields, near Cork, and was about thirteen years old. His voyage on the *Mary Russell* was his first, and it was a trial to see if he was fit to be taken on as apprentice. He recounted the facts of the return voyage as we know them. It is from Scully's testimony that we learn that he and Deaves pleaded for Captain Stewart to spare the life of John Howes, while Richards struck Howes in the skull with the axe in three places. This led to Captain Stewart praising Richards for being a clever fellow, and telling him he would get 100 guineas for saving the ship and be a gentleman all his life. Scully said he and Deaves acted as they did through terror that, if they disobeyed, Captain Stewart would kill them. Deaves was at the wheel when the ship that had responded to their distress signal went away for a second time, and he tried to follow her, but the *Mary Russell*, under reduced sail, could not go fast enough to overtake her. This was the point at which Captain Stewart decided that his men were under 'the curse of God', and he summoned Scully and Richards below, leaving Deaves at the wheel.

It is from Scully's testimony that we learn that Scully, Richards and Thomas Hammond witnessed the killings. He also describes how 'Master Hammond', as he calls him, ran and untied the three boys when Captain Callendar and his crew got on board. His conclusion was 'Captain Stewart had no reason for the murder but suspicion and dreams; there was not even impertinence to the captain and witness has heard the men say they would not allow a hair of his head to be hurt; six of the sufferers were married and have left widows and families to mourn their loss. Captain Stewart had no sign of drunkenness when he committed the act.'

The next to make his deposition was the first mate, William Smith, still displaying untended the wounds to his head, eye and ear that he had received in the lazarette. Smith was identified as a native of Scotland, and stated that he had joined the *Mary Russell* in the Cove of Cork about four months previously for a voyage to Barbados and back. Smith outlined the story of the journey home to Cork, starting with the dream that Stewart had told him about a week or so out of Barbados. Smith told of his attempts to discourage his captain from believing in the power of dreams, and Stewart's continued insistence that it was Almighty God warning

154

him. The courtroom remained in hushed silence as Smith spoke of the charts and navigation instruments being thrown overboard, and the incidents of the night he was on watch, going up and down to the nail locker because of the troublesome binnacle lamp. Then Smith described the tying up of his shipmates, and their final moments of life, as seen by him from the lazarette through a hole in the floor.

The next to be sworn in was John Howes, and once again his battered and bloodied appearance, unchanged since the events of the previous weekend, impressed the onlookers: 'The appearance of this witness produced a painful sensation; he was dreadfully mutilated, and his clothes bore evident marks of the horrible slaughter which he had escaped.' (*Freeman's Journal*, 2 July, 1828). Howes' deposition confirmed the facts as outlined by Scully and Smith, and made it clear that there had been no plans for mutiny except in the deranged belief of Captain Stewart. Even in the indirect speech in which Howes' words are conveyed by the reporter, as was the convention in those days, his voice comes through as that of a man with clear ideas of right and wrong. Howes, just before he lets himself be tied, is sitting on a seat on deck with his captain near the windlass, complaining about

Stewart's bizarre behaviour in tying up all the men in the cabin, something Howes had never seen before on board ship:

The Captain admitted it, but he said there were two or three of the men tied in the cabin who acknowledged piracy, and begged pardon. Witness asked who these were, and he [Captain Stewart] said Captain Raynes and Tim Connell; witness mentioned if they declared piracy, they kept him ignorant of it, and he knew nothing of it, and if he thought witness guilty, to shoot him dead at once, as he had him then in his power; Stewart said he had no wish for that, as he wished to carry witness, above all men, in a whole skin to Cork. Witness told him he had no right to treat people so, and that he wished a British Man of War would heave in sight, and he would not be cutting such capers over poor defenceless people; he [Stewart] said he wished there was [a British Man-of-War in sight], and he wished to secure witness, as he was a resolute man, and a clever fellow, to which witness replied it did not appear so, by allowing himself to be tied . . .

Later, when Howes, still tied, was moved in to the shelter of the half-deck, the captain sat with him for about three hours, during which time he appeared to be 'very familiar' with the witness, mocking the bad English of Swanson the Swede and Morley the Irish speaker, and also mocking them for being so frightened: 'Witness said it was foolish for Swanson to be frightened, as he need dread nothing if he had a good conscience.'

Howes in his deposition goes to pains to make it clear that the boys, particularly John Deaves and Daniel Scully, were not acting on their own initiative, but were being both bullied and bribed by the captain. He recounts his tussle with Captain Stewart, the two shooting incidents, and his escape, wounded, into the forepeak. Howes only heard of the fate of his shipmates when he and Smith encountered each other in the forepeak:

The mate made his escape out of the lazarette, and spoke to witness through the hold, on hearing him coughing and striking a light [for his pipe, presumably]; he said he had made his escape after the Captain had cut one of his ears off, and knocked one of his eyes out, and that he was half-dead; witness asked how the rest of the crew got on, and he said that Captain Stewart had murdered the whole of them, and expected that [i.e. Captain Stewart believed that] he [Smith] was dead also. Witness mentioned to Smith that if the Captain attempted to scuttle the ship, and to take himself and the boys away in the boat, he would endeavour with the axe to cut away the long boat for their escape.

Howes finishes his deposition with this conclusion:

The Captain's mind must have been disturbed, but he saw no reason for it; witness is at a loss to tell what reason he would have for his conduct; it would not be for interest, or spite, or for credit; he appeared melancholy at times, so that Connell asked him once why he appeared so down-hearted.

The only one of the three people to make depositions to the Coroner's court to mention directly that he sometimes thought Captain Stewart was 'out of his senses' was the child Thomas Hammond. Described by the newspaper as 'an intelligent child', the eleven-year-old first had to convince the Coroner that he understood the serious implications of speaking under oath, which he did with ease. This is the child's deposition as

158

it would read in his own voice, without the distortion of being reported as above, in the third person:

I am the son of Mr James Hammond, and we live at Cottage, near Cove. I was sent to the West Indies for the benefit of my health, and returned in the *Mary Russell* with Captain Stewart. The Captain was quite pleasant going out, but on his coming home he was different. He told me had had a great suspicion of Captain Raynes because of some dream he had, which had made him think Captain Raynes and the crew would take the vessel from him. I saw nothing about the crew to make me suspect that anything like that was going on.

Captain Stewart called Captain Raynes and the mate down to take a glass of grog, and he said to him 'Captain Raynes, if you do not drop the intimacy with my crew, and stop speaking to them in Irish, I will throw my log-lines and reels overboard.' Captain Raynes was in the habit of associating with the crew, and he used to wash and shave himself forward. Captain Raynes said he liked to hear them talk Irish. He said he was sorry for offending the Captain, and that if he knew it was offending him, he wouldn't have done it.

Captain Stewart did not take off his clothes to go to sleep. He took little rest for the remainder of the voyage, and he would never go to sleep without having a man or a boy watching him. The first thing that made him have someone keep watch while he slept was when a pocket knife was missing which belonged to one of the men. The Captain said it was taken for the purpose of killing him, though it was afterwards found.

I was in the main cabin with the boys when the murder was being committed. Daniel Scully cried, and I thought my life was not worth a pin. The Captain took an oath, and said that if I or any of the boys changed colour [changed sides to support the men], he would shoot us. I was in my berth in the main cabin all this time. I was in the cabin when they were brought down, and not a single man of them made any resistance. It seemed they let themselves be tied up to satisfy Captain Stewart, to calm him down. Mr Raynes said, when he was asked if he would let himself be tied, 'To be sure, Sir'. The Captain used to loosen some of them occasionally, but then he fastened them up tightly again.

I was locked into the stateroom with the boys and the Captain and we slept a little.

Captain Raynes complained on Saturday night of the tightness of the rope; but on Sunday the Captain lashed them all firmly on the deck of the cabin and drove staples in. Connell and Keating begged me to ask the Captain to spare their lives. When he came down after firing at Howes, I pleaded with him to have no more bloodshed. He said would not, if he could help it: if Howes submitted to be lashed, there would be no more bloodshed, the Captain said, walking and strutting about the cabin: 'I'll show them what William Stewart can do, and I'll let them see I'll not jump out of the cabin window'. Some of the men cried out to be spared while he was killing the others, and I called out to spare some of them at all events, to bring home the vessel; the mate in particular, who was locked down in the lazarette.

The Captain often told me that the men wanted to take away the vessel, but when I asked him to spare the men's lives, he laughed at me. He said he knew what he was doing, and if they escaped they would murder me, himself and the boys. The Captain used to lie down for about half an hour and then start and moan; when he did sleep it was always disturbed. I used to think sometimes he was out of his mind.

When this child concluded his testimony, the jury intimated to the Coroner that there was no necessity for going further into the investigation. The jury retired for a few minutes and returned with the following verdict:

That the several Sailors and Passengers were killed by the hands of Capt Stewart, being then and for some days before in a state of mental derangement.

13

After the Inquest

Only when the inquest was over, late in the evening on Friday 27 June 1828, were John Howes and William Smith taken to the North Infirmary in Cork to have their wounds attended to. We learn this from a letter that Coroner Henry Hardy wrote on Saturday 28 June, the day after the inquest, to William Gregory (1762–1840), Under Secretary to the Lord Lieutenant, Richard Wellesley, at Dublin Castle. (William Gregory's grandson, Sir William Henry Gregory (1817–1892) was Governor of Ceylon, and his second wife Augusta, Lady Gregory, was the founder of the Abbey Theatre.) Hardy asked Gregory to bring his letter's contents to the attention of the Lord Lieutenant. He enclosed the detailed report of the inquest that had appeared that morning in the *Constitution*, stating that it was in his opinion 'a very full and in substance correct account of the proceedings'. This ensured that the Lord Lieutenant in Dublin would know the details of the shocking and unprecedented case before the *Freeman's Journal* broke the story in Dublin on 2 July.

The letter adds some details that did not appear in the newspapers, as they were not part of the evidence given at the inquest. We learn that Captain Callendar had sailed for Belfast; the mate Smith was allowed home to his wife and family who lived in Cove; John Howes remained in the North Infirmary 'for cure', and the other witnesses 'are here', meaning it would seem, that the boys Scully, Deaves and Richards were being held in custody at the Bridewell, pending a trial. (Cork city's Bridewell was at the junction of Cornmarket and Kyrl's Street on the site of today's Garda Station. It was used as a house of detention for a variety of prisoners, from vagrants and prostitutes to debtors and vagabonds).

Then the Coroner writes that the Mayor has asked him to tell the Attorney General about a passage in the letter received from the Inspector in Skibbereen which the Mayor did not permit to be read out in court 'for obvious reasons'. The passage in question states that 'William Stewart charges William Smith, one of the wounded men of his brig, with the murder of a marine on board the *Lopara* frigate when she lay in the Downs . . . [illegible line] made his escape'.

There is no record of any frigate named the *Lopara* in the Royal Navy at the time, but given that this is a third-hand account from the lips of a deeply disturbed man who has just killed seven men, the frigate's name could have got garbled in the telling.

On 30 June Captain Stewart was brought from Skibbereen to Cork County Gaol, as the *Constitution* reported on 1 July:

COMMITTAL OF CAPTAIN STEWART LATE OF THE *Mary Russell*

This wretched man, whose hands are imbued with the blood of so many human beings, arrived in this City yesterday in a chaise from Skibbereen where he had been in custody for several days, and was immediately committed to the County Gaol, under a County Magistrate's warrant. He is a man of small stature and rather thin and pale in the face, with a sharp quick eye. As far as we can learn the man appears in a sane and tranquil state of mind, and has spoken of the tragedy in which he has been the principal with apparent indifference. Some of his observations on this head have been given to us, but for obvious reasons we forbear from giving them publicity.

165

The newspaper then refers to Captain Stewart's concerns about his wife, who was heavily pregnant. It is hard to imagine the horror of the ordeal that Betsy Stewart had been experiencing since she first heard that all was not well aboard the *Mary Russell*: her husband was not on board, having jumped overboard off Cape Clear and been picked up by a fishing boat. Seven members of the crew had been murdered, and it was being said that they had been killed by her husband.

As a captain's wife, Betsy was among the elite in this seafaring town, living in a fine four-storey house looking directly south over the harbour. For the past ten days or more whenever she looked out of the window to check the new arrivals, she had reason to hope that one of the brigs sailing up from Roche's Point would be the *Mary Russell*, with her husband on board. She was anxious in case the hot climate should have a bad effect on his head, as had happened to him once before. But this time she hoped all would be well, and he would arrive before the birth of their fifth child, whose time was coming ever nearer, and once again enjoy the company of his four existing children: Henry (ten), Francis (seven), Margaret Jane (five), and Timothy (two). The mate William Smith's wife and children also lived in Cove.

166

Smith had been chosen as mate because he had sailed with Stewart before. While they may not have been close friends, Mrs Smith and Betsy Stewart would be known to each other in such a small community. Moreover, they shared the bond of their husbands being on a long sea voyage together as captain and mate, out of contact with their home base for over three months.

One can only hope that the Stewart family had staunch friends in their local community to stand by poor Betsy and comfort her as the facts were revealed. The Hammond family, whose child had just been returned to them after giving evidence at the inquest, would have been as shocked as Betsy to hear the terrible news about their friend William Stewart.

The report from the *Constitution* for 1 July describing Captain Stewart's arrival in Cork, continues:

He [Captain Stewart] has expressed great solicitude about his wife, whose situation since the lamentable intelligence reached her has been most precarious. She was far advanced in a state of pregnancy, and within the last few days we understand she was visited with premature *accouchment*, and was delivered of a dead child!

This report is an example of the kind of hysteria that surrounded anything to do with the murdering sea captain at that time. A child of Captain Stewart and Betsy Stewart was baptised Eliza at St Colman's (Catholic) Church, Cove on 1 December 1828. This fact contradicts the newspaper report, and confirms that the child Betsy was carrying was born alive, but not baptised until some months later.

However, the continuing burden on Betsy must have been immense. From being the wife of a popular sea captain, she became, literally overnight, the wife of a monster and mass murderer. As well as Mrs Smith, the wife of the mate who survived, albeit badly injured, some of the murdered men, all of whom were living in the Cork area, probably had family in Cove, and they certainly had friends and supporters among the seafaring community there and in Passage West.

Betsy Stewart knew that whatever the outcome of the trial, her husband's career was over, and she and her children would be without any means of support. Overnight she had gone from a position of prosperity and security to being the wife of a man accused of mass murder, and imprisoned while awaiting trial. Overnight she and her children had gone from a comfortable, secure life to face an uncertain future, most likely one of poverty and social ostracism.

When times were more prosperous, William Stewart would never have agreed to take the *Mary Russell* to Barbados. There are records of him having turned down similar voyages, on the grounds that the warm climate did not suit his health. Both he and Betsy knew that he sometimes suffered from strange states of mind, and believed (as was common at the time) that his mental condition was made worse by hot weather. But by 1828, work was scarce, and the family needed the money: he could not turn down a lucrative voyage. His decision had cost him his health and his reputation, it had put his family in a highly precarious financial situation, and it had cost seven good men their lives.

The *Constitution* considers the victims and their families in the same report on 1 July:

The situation of those families into whose recesses he [Captain Stewart] carried death and misery is truly deplorable. The mother of young Mr Sullivan is inconsolable, and it is thought will scarcely survive the shock; and the family and friends of Captain Raynes, who was generally respected and esteemed, are equally distressed and afflicted. But what must be the pitiable

169

state of those families who were in indigent circumstances, and depended on the ill-fated victims for support — it would be difficult to portray. This subject, however, has been taken up warmly by the citizens of Cork, who are ever alive to the dictates of humanity — and we hope and trust it will be attended with good effects, as far as pecuniary assistance will go.

The Lord Mayor and the high sheriffs of the City of Cork invited subscriptions to a fund for the relief of the families of Captain Stewart's victims. By early August the fund totalled £163 8s 6d. The largest donation, £21, came from the owners of the *Mary Russell*. The Corporation of the City gave £10, and its officials gave £1 each, as did Henry Sharpe, the doctor at the inquest. Some donors were anonymous, others came from the leading merchants, including William Crawford Jnr, and Mrs Beamish of Beaumont. One of the smaller donations, five shillings, came from a journalist, Mr Barry of the *Southern Reporter*.

A second report on the fund, carried on 2 August, under the headline *Unparalleled Distress and Affliction*, mentions that five families had been deprived of their sole means of support by 'the most unfortunate and melancholy catastrophe which occurred on board the Brig *Mary Russell* on her voyage from Barbados'. It adds that the two surviving crew members are so badly wounded that their families also deserve financial aid. Six weeks after the events that caused their wounds, Smith and Howes were still unable to return to work.

There is no record of any donation from the *Constitution*, though newspaper offices acted as collection points, as well as the Mayor and high sheriffs' offices. Newspapers did well out of the massive scandal and the public's appetite for details. The *Constitution* printed several hundred above their usual number for the issue carrying the inquest, and demand was still not satisfied. They considered publishing a special edition 'with additions to the distressing facts', which would be 'worthy of being preserved in every family throughout the United Kingdom'.

14

The *Mary Russell* in Cork

The inquest was concluded on Friday 27 June, and at the beginning of the next week the *Mary Russell* was moved from Cove to Cork city centre. Having discharged part of her cargo at Passage West, in order to be able to navigate up the river, the rest of her cargo was being unloaded at Custom House Quay, in front of a crowd of curious onlookers, keen for a glimpse of 'the ship of seven murders'.

The Custom House was built in 1818 at the eastern end of George's Street (today's Oliver Plunkett Street). It was designed in a severely classical style. Its central front had a pediment, which in 1828 bore the Royal Arms. (Today it is the headquarters of the Port of Cork Authority.) From the seaward approach, it lies at the apex of the island on which Cork's city centre stands, at the point where the River Lee divides into two channels. Behind it was the Custom House Yard, serried ranks of warehouses, built from limestone and sandstone, with high gable ends. This was the central depot for incoming cargo, and also the place where cargos were gathered prior to shipping. Here the Barbados sugar and the hides on board the *Mary Russell* would be stored before being sold at auction. Across the water, on the recently completed Penrose Quay, stood the offices of the St George Steam Packet Company, which was rapidly becoming the focus of the city's marine activities.

It was only a short walk from the Custom House to the South Mall, the commercial centre of Cork. South Mall, Grand Parade, St Patrick's Street and the Cornmarket, previously waterways, had been filled in during the late eighteenth century, and turned into fine wide streets, which were lit by gas from the mid-1820s. The Commercial Buildings on South Mall had a magnificent coffee room, 60 feet long, which was the hub of the city's mercantile community. Here the merchants would congregate to read the newspapers, and to hear the latest news. The Buildings provided a suitably dignified venue for merchant meetings, and facilities for the all-important auctions of cargo. It advertised itself as being 'open to military and naval officers, and to all strangers'. The Imperial Clarence Hotel in South Mall was under the same ownership, and offered facilities for families and commercial travellers. Captain

James Goold Raynes would have been well known in these circles, as would Captain Stewart. The majority of Cork city's merchants were Catholic or Quaker. This was one of few professions open to those whose beliefs prevented them from taking the oath of allegiance to the British Crown. The Catholics could not take such an oath because it contradicted their religious beliefs, while members of the Religious Society of Friends (as the Quakers are more properly known) did not believe in taking oaths of any kind, as it contradicted their belief that one should tell the truth at all times. However, the city's mayors and sheriffs, and the members of its council were still drawn from the Protestant elite. Since the mid-eighteenth century, Cork Corporation had been controlled by a group of wealthy Protestant families, whose names — Perrier, Bresnard, Gibbings, Newsom, Dorman, Wrixon, Busteed — recur over and over again in its records.

The military presence in the Cork district was under the command of Sir George Bingham from 1827 to 1832. He had previously been senior officer of the garrison that accompanied Napoleon to St Helena. Sir George was known for his tact and kindliness, and generally held in high esteem. He is also listed among the donors (£1) to the relief fund for the victims of the tragedy aboard the *Mary Russell*.

Mr and Mrs Hall, whose lively account of their 1840 visit to Ireland, was quoted earlier, approvingly remarked on the abundance of 'Institutions — charitable, scientific and literary' — in Cork city. In the summer of 1828 the Cork Society for Promoting the Fine Arts held an exhibition at the Saloon of Arts on St Patrick's Street, home of the Mechanics' Institute. This consisted of some 113 original works of art by 34 artists, but the chief talking point of the exhibition was a death mask of Napoleon. This had been taken the morning after his death, and was placed on show, 'for the gratification of the public curiosity, so naturally excited by it'. (*Cork Constitution*). Napoleon, or Boney, as he was also called, had long been a bogeyman figure, used to frighten children into obeying their parents. The exhibition closed to the public on 10 July 1828. By then there was a new bogeyman to arouse the public curiosity: Captain William Stewart of the ship of seven murders.

★ ★ ★

One of the first visitors to the now infamous brig at Custom House Quay, and the only one to leave a record of what he found, was the ever-curious William Scoresby. This obsessive interest in the *Mary Russell* may seem strange for a man on his honeymoon, but Scoresby is mirroring his behaviour on his 'marriage tour' (honeymoon) after his first wedding. In 1811 the 22-year-old sea captain had married Mary Eliza Lockwood. The two-month marriage tour began with a visit to a friend of Mary Eliza's in Cumberland, who was paymaster of Stanhope Mills, lead mines belonging to Greenwich Hospital. Scoresby occupied himself visiting the mines, and making detailed notes about their workings, output and labour conditions. In his biography (Whitby, 1975) Tom and Cordelia Stamp comment:

His was a restless mind, driven by a force which compelled him to observe and record each slight detail of whatever happened to be under his notice at the time. Throughout his whole life this attention to minute detail, so characteristic of the scientific mind, persisted, and is very evident in the immense pile of paper he left. The tour of Stanhope Mills was followed by a visit to the Vale of Whitfield. 'There are no mines in the vicinity of Whitfield,' he wrote. Did the young bride heave a sigh of relief?

William Scoresby was able to roam the cabin and deck of the *Mary Russell* at his leisure, and confesses that he found it unusually exciting to be in the very place where such terrible things had happened so recently. It was, he concludes, almost like having been there at the time. The cabin, which he measured carefully, had been cleared of the bodies and what the scientist terms 'their more offensive extravasations', but the floor was still bloodstained. In it Scoresby could clearly see the places where the nails and staples securing the prisoners had been hammered in. The hole broken through the floor above the lazarette to allow the chief mate Smith to breathe was still unrepaired.

At every step he encountered 'objects and places of melancholy interest' that had featured in the story he had heard from the lips of Smith, Howes and the boys. He saw the granes carried by one of the captain's 'three youthful abettors', and the axes and the crowbar. He saw the blood-spattered case of books that Howes had used as a shield against his captain's pistol shot. In the half-deck, where Captain Stewart and Howes had wrestled hand-to-hand for their lives, the hammock and its bedding used by the chief mate, Smith, still hung. Most macabre of all, the sugar-casks that formed the floor of the half-deck still showed abundant traces of the blood which had been shed there.

The passage from the cabin to the deck, the location of the nail locker that Smith had visited three times the night before the tying up of the men began, and which Stewart had barricaded against Howes during the night after the killings, Scoresby found was 'rendered interesting by the circumstances connected with it'. Scoresby also mentions, without naming names, the presence of one of the surviving men (Smith, we presume, as Howes was still in the North Infirmary), and one of the boys (unnamed). They were there to help with the unloading, in the absence of the captain and all the other men in his crew who had loaded the cargo in Barbados.

Scoresby found that being in the actual place where the murders had happened, surrounded by the objects with which the crime was carried out, in the presence of two survivors of the event, brought the whole drama to life in his imagination. He experienced sensations of dismay and horror 'so vivid as to be only exceeded by the actual witnessing of the original dreadful scenes'.

Despite the tragedy associated with her, the *Mary Russell* was quickly put back to work.

On 26 July, the *Constitution* ran an advertisement announcing the departure of 'the fine, first class brig, *Mary Russell*, Peter Newman, Commander' in the first week of August for St John's, Newfoundland. 'For freight or passage, apply to Deaves Brothers, Lapp's Island'. She was back in Cork with a cargo of fish on 1 November. On the same page as the advertisement of her departure for Newfoundland, the auction of her cargo of '50 Hogsheads and Tierces, Bright and Middling Barbados Sugars, recently landed' is advertised for one o'clock on Tuesday 29 July.

While the Coroner's inquest was under way, Captain Stewart had been taken to the county gaol where he was to await trial. The Cork County Gaol, whose massive Doric façade now forms part of the Science Building at University College, Cork, was built in 1791 and rebuilt and extended in 1818 to relieve the appalling conditions and overcrowding. Its grounds extended from the riverside site northwest to the road now known as College Road. The building of Great George's Street (now Washington Street) and its extension, New Road (Western Road) in 1824, gave direct access to the gaol from the city centre. To reach it, a single-arch bridge was built across a channel of the River

Lee, and an imposing new entrance was built, based on the Temple of Bacchus in Athens. This consisted of four columns surmounted by a portico. The new gaol was one of the city's finest public buildings at the time. It had a central block, with two detached wings, and three other ranges of three-storey buildings radiating from the centre northwards. The central block contained the governor's apartments on the ground floor, a chapel for Catholics and Protestants on the second floor, and an infirmary on the third floor. The prisoners were clothed in prison garb, and kept occupied on the tread wheel, which supplied the prison with water, or whitewashing and cleaning the floors of the yards and passages. By 1835 almost 1,000 prisoners were housed in the gaol. The emphasis was on reformation of prisoners, an unusually enlightened regime for the time. Captain Stewart was given a cell to himself.

The degree of interest and excitement caused by the presence of the murderer of seven men in the county gaol caused the institution 'no small measure of inconvenience', with crowds gathering outside the massive gate, in the hope of having a glimpse of the monster.

15

Meetings with a Murderer

On Saturday 5 July, a few days after his visit to the *Mary Russell* at Custom House Quay, William Scoresby, through a friend who was on the Gaol Committee, managed to get permission to visit Captain Stewart in prison. Scoresby's friend lived near Cove, and was well known to Captain Stewart, who welcomed his friend's visit and received him kindly. This suggests that some at least of the Stewarts' friends and neighbours were standing by the family. William Scoresby, however, was not initially welcome, as he recalls:

But on me, being a total stranger, he looked with an eye of suspicious objection, evidently considering my presence intrusive. My friend, however, having made me known to him in such a way as to remove the impression of my visit being intended in idle curiosity, he at length permitted me to enter his cell, where, the jailor having left us, we spent nearly a couple of hours, whilst he related to us, with increasing confidence and openness, the leading circumstances of the fatal voyage.

Captain Stewart, as a prisoner facing a murder charge and a devout Christian, was probably more impressed by Scoresby's status as an ordained minister than by his maritime accomplishments, but the combination was a fortunate one. The presence of someone who understood both the nautical and the religious aspects of Stewart's situation must have been a great comfort to the captain. Scoresby was fourteen years younger than the 53-year-old Stewart, but had had a far more distinguished career. The two men took to each other immediately. This first meeting, almost two weeks to the day since Captain Stewart had restrained and killed seven men single-handedly, was the start of a long friendship, sustained by two more visits and continued by correspondence. This is Scoresby's description of Stewart at that first meeting:

There was an evident candour of manner which convinced us that he felt himself justified in all he had done. For whilst he avowed himself ready to meet his trial, he declared himself prepared to establish the *necessity* of the act which he had committed.

Unless it were a certain sharpness of expression in the eye, and quickness of manner, we perceived scarcely any other indications that the person before us was of unsound mind. He seemed to be in the full possession of all his ordinary faculties.

Stewart's account of the voyage was told with such consistency, attention to detail and apparent accuracy, that Scoresby admits that, if Stewart's suspicions of mutiny had been better grounded in reality, then one would have been tempted to excuse, on grounds of self-preservation, much of his treatment of his crew.

The more he looked at Stewart the more astonished Scoresby was at the fact that Stewart was so evidently inferior in strength to the muscle-power of the seven individuals he had killed. Even the most powerful of men, reflected Scoresby, might have dismissed the possibility of killing seven men at once as 'apparently impracticable'. This is what he saw when he looked at Stewart:

His figure appeared slight, and below the middle stature, but evidently smart and agile. With features somewhat sharp, complexion fair, hair red, and a profile straight and indicative of intelligence, he exhibited a moral physiognomy not so much characteristic of anything bad or repulsive, as of a temperament excitable, ardent and passionate. The fire of the eye, and quickness of movement in the body, to which I have already alluded, were the only apparent characteristics which struck me as being peculiar.

Scoresby admits to what he calls 'peculiar emotions', on being in the presence of someone who had single-handedly killed seven of his fellow men:

Feelings of repulsion and distrust were forcibly excited by being locked up with a man who had been the agent of such a terrific slaughter; and it was not without shuddering from the very heart that I received, at the close of this first interview, the now freely offered, but not obtruded [thrust forward forcibly] murderous hand.

Even though he was in Cork to celebrate his wedding, the case of Captain Stewart seemed to follow William Scoresby around, a symptom, perhaps of the general public's interest in the case during those days. For a few days later Scoresby and his wife Elizabeth were paying a visit to her brother-in-law,

Captain Hoare RN. Captain Hoare was also a member of the Gaol Committee, and while the Scoresbys were with him, a message arrived from Captain Stewart, requesting an audience with Captain Hoare to discuss his case and give his opinion as to whether his act was justified given that he supposed a mutiny was intended. Scoresby must have asked to accompany Captain Hoare. Thus it was that he gained admittance to Stewart's cell for a second time, in spite of a strict prohibition by the magistrates against the admission of any visitors. Captain Hoare and Reverend Scoresby found Captain Stewart in the common room of his ward, writing a detailed account of the events on board the *Mary Russell* for his uncle, the Reverend Dr Stewart of Kilgarriffe, Clonakilty. William Stewart led his visitors to the privacy of his own cell, where he read this letter aloud to them. It was a long letter, and Scoresby found that it was written with great clarity and consistency, and had the ring of truth and accuracy in everything except Stewart's notion of an impending mutiny.

Stewart spoke to Scoresby and Hoare for nearly two hours, detailing in chronological order the various events of the voyage from Barbados to Cork, especially those which had a bearing on the fatal tragedy. He emphasised

185

particularly the incidents of behaviour among his crew that had made him suspect that a mutiny was planned.

Stewart began by blaming Captain Raynes, whom he took on board from charitable motives at Barbados, who was 'the cause of the whole'. Stewart accused Raynes of 'getting at' the men, to stir up a mutiny. He went on to say that once the chief mate, William Smith, had admitted to being engaged in 'a daring transaction' (the murder on board the frigate), he lost all confidence in him. He could not trust John Howes, he said, because Howes had sailed in a better situation (as a chief or second mate), and was discontented at being on board as a seaman. He had caught Smith the mate, who denied all knowledge of celestial navigiation, taking an observation of the moon, and regarded his hiding that knowledge as being part of his mutinous plan. But his chief suspect was Captain Raynes:

Captain Raynes, who was in disgrace at home, had no desire to return, and having lost his situation both as captain and mate, he could have no hopes of a ship. I suspected him, therefore, that he wanted to turn pirate: and when I threw overboard the charts and log-line, I marked his confusion and disappointment.

186

His visitors then questioned Captain Stewart about why he had found it necessary to kill his prisoners when they were so securely tied up as to be unlikely to be able to take revenge on him. The crux of the matter lay with the failure of the second vessel that approached the *Mary Russell* to come to his aid. Stewart said:

My hopes of relief had been greatly excited by the near approach of the second vessel which we saw on Sunday afternoon. But when she bore away, the disappointment was *unbearable*. I considered it as Providence indicating that the prisoners were guilty, and designed for death.

From these and other considerations, Stewart confessed, his mind was 'wrought up to a state of reckless despair'. He dreaded the revenge of Howes, who was still on the loose in the hold, and who had sworn he would take Stewart's life. He could see night coming on, which would expose him to sudden attacks. He was so worn out from fatigue, anxiety and lack of rest that he could no longer keep his eyes open. He was suspicious of the loyalty of the boys, one of whom, he believed, must have loosened Howes' bonds, as Howes had been tied up more strongly

187

than any of the rest. He was afraid that the boys would free the other prisoners while he slept, so he saw no alternative but putting them all to death, or being killed himself, the victim of their revenge. He concluded:

> *Therefore, I was under the necessity of killing them* [Scoresby's italics]. But, if that fellow Howes had not been adrift in the hold, I would not have put them to death; but I was afraid of him.

After finishing his statement, and exhausting every possible argument as to why it was absolutely necessary for him to kill the seven men, Stewart anxiously asked Captain Hoare for his opinion.

Captain Hoare was candid in his reply, saying that even if the intention to mutiny, which he judged to be imagined rather than real, could be proved, he still did not think that the killings could be justified, especially considering how carefully and thoroughly the men had been tied up. Scoresby's account continues:

> Stewart seemed greatly disappointed and affected, anxiously exclaiming 'I'm sorry for it! I'm very sorry for it!' [i.e. he was sorry that Captain Hoare did not think the

killings could be justified.] He still, however, persisted in his own conviction 'that he was compelled by necessity to commit the act'. But he once avowed that 'when he thought of the sixth Commandment, he felt some misgivings of conscience'.

The sixth Commandment is Thou Shalt Not Kill.

As Captain Hoare and the Reverend Scoresby were leaving the prisoner's ward, they found 'his almost heart-broken wife', waiting for them to come out so that she could visit her husband. The visit would have involved a journey of almost two hours from Cove. Writes Scoresby: 'We spoke to her as we passed, and truly sympathized with her deep-seated, remediless grief.' Scoresby here interpolates a short sermon, addressed to the 'poor sufferer', recognising that whether her husband is condemned to death, or allowed to live, to her the verdict will only speak sorrow. Unfortunately for our curiosity, Scoresby was too much of a gentleman to mention whether Mrs Stewart was still heavily pregnant on 5 July, or whether she had recently given birth.

Scoresby's preoccupation with the ship of seven murders so soon after his marriage does not seem to have had any long-term

189

ill-effect on the relationship. Even though the course of their marriage was not a conventionally smooth one, the couple remained devoted to each other for the next nineteen years. Elizabeth Fitzgerald of Corkbegg was troubled by poor health from the start, and could not settle in Liverpool, even after the couple had moved house from the docks to a more salubrious quarter near the Botanic Garden. Scoresby's youngest son from his first marriage, a delicate, rather whimsical child called Frederick, born in 1818, who had been unusually close to his father since he was widowed, admitted he had trouble 'loving' his stepmother: he greatly resented her, and the attention paid to her by his father. Elizabeth spent more and more time at Corkbegg instead of in Liverpool, eventually moving back entirely until her husband should find a new parish. They were reunited after four years spent largely apart when he took charge of Bedford Chapel in Exeter, the central building in an elegant crescent of new houses. In 1839, Scoresby, now a Doctor of Divinity, was appointed Vicar of Bradford, a difficult posting, as most of the people in the manufacturing town were dissenters who shunned the Established Church. The cause of Elizabeth's death in December 1847 is not known, but she had been ill for some time before, 'in a state of health and under a disease which did not, in her case, render life desirable', as her husband wrote. Scoresby was in America on a lecture tour when she died, and had been expecting this news, which arrived six weeks after the event. Having recovered from his initial distress, he wrote a touching eulogy, praising her intelligent piety, deep humility, feminine delicacy, purity of mind and integrity and holiness of life.

16

News Travels

The outrage at the immensity of Captain Stewart's crime spread from Cork as the news travelled, to Dublin, London, and around the known world. The London *Times* first broke the news of the ship of seven murders on 1 July under the headline 'Extraordinary Story'. On 2 July 1828 *The Times* carried a full report of the inquest, attributed to the *Southern Reporter*, relating events that had taken place the previous Friday 27 June.

News travelling was still a literal term in these pretelegraph days. Newspapers were carried on board ship and, by the time they reached their destination the 'news' they contained was, in the case of transatlantic destinations, at least six weeks old.

Part of the fascination with the ship of seven murders lay in the violent and extreme nature of the crime — the murder of seven innocent men — and how this contrasted with the respectability of the murderer: a middle-aged, Protestant sea captain of good reputation, with a wife and family, and an uncle a rector and a member of the landed gentry (Reverend Dr Henry Wilson Stewart LLD of Tannies Cottage, Kilgarriffe, Clonakilty). If the crime had been committed by a low-life ruffian it would not have attracted such attention. For example, a report from the *Limerick Chronicle* of 30 June 1828 was reprinted in a Quebec newspaper around 18 August 1828 under the heading: 'Deplorable and Melancholy Catastrophe'. The *Limerick Chronicle* report, having described the events in broad outline, concludes 'We cannot conceive that anything but insanity could induce a human being to imbue his hands in the blood of seven fellow creatures under circumstances so horrible as the above represents'.

The Quebec newspaper added this comment: 'Captain Stewart of the *Mary Russell*, is known here, as having commanded both the *Sir James Kempt* and the *Albion*, engaged in the Irish trade. He must have been under the influence of insanity to have committed such a cold blooded and horrible act.'

What fascinated people was how Captain Stewart had managed to convince seven able-bodied men, one after another, to be tied up and rendered helpless. People puzzled over why he should kill them with a crowbar when they no longer represented any threat to him, being bound hand and foot. Note too the importance attached to rank at the time, how Captain Raynes is set apart from the common sailors — six seamen and a naval gentleman. And finally, in Quebec just as in Limerick, there is the warm expression of hope that such an act was carried out while 'under the influence of insanity', because for a sane man to kill seven of his fellow men while they were bound and unable to cause him harm is a 'cold blooded and terrible act', wicked beyond comprehension.

The question of whether Captain Stewart was mad when he committed the murders or not was to become the pivotal issue at his trial. The Coroner's inquest had reached the verdict 'That the several Sailors and Passengers were killed by the hands of Captain Stewart, being then, and for some days before, in a state of mental derangement'.

William Scoresby observed that while the chief ground for assuming that there was something wrong with Captain Stewart's mind lay in his insistence on the mutinous intentions of his passengers and crew, none of the survivors ever mentioned any suspicions that Stewart might be mad — or deranged, as was the favoured term at the time. The only person to accuse him directly of madness was the child Thomas Hammond, who lived at close quarters with Captain Stewart for the whole voyage, a fact which Scoresby missed. The report of Hammond's evidence to the Coroner's inquest ends, 'He appeared to be disturbed, and used to start up with his eyes half open; witness thought sometimes that the Captain was out of his senses.'

Scoresby says if the men aboard the *Mary Russell* had seriously considered that Captain Stewart was of unsound mind, then why would they have so promptly obeyed his extraordinary orders for reducing sail and heaving-to, when they had a favourable wind, and were almost home? He goes on to ask whether the men would have agreed to be bound, without any threats having been made, if they had thought Stewart mad? Would the captain of the *Mary Harriet* have supplied him with pistols for his defence against a mutinous crew if he had noticed anything that might suggest that Stewart was mad?

Scoresby states that he does not intend to cast any doubt on the verdict of the Coroner's court by asking these questions: he is simply reporting the questions that people were asking each other in Cork on first hearing of the unprecedented events on the ship of seven murders. He reports that, among the people he spent time with, the general conclusion was that if anyone was deranged aboard the *Mary Russell*, it was the nine strong men who allowed themselves to be tied up by a single man of inferior strength to all of them: 'These, if any must have been the madmen!' he concludes, the feeble joke representing the baffled incomprehension with which the tragic event was viewed by many.

In the six and a half weeks that intervened between the inquest and the trial of Captain Stewart, debate raged in the homes and coffee houses of Cork — and Dublin, London and the rest of Britain. The talk centred on the main issue, that of Captain Stewart's state of mind: was Captain Stewart really mad, or was he just faking it to escape a verdict of murder, and the consequent death sentence? And if he was mad, why did his crew not realise this, and restrain him, instead of vice versa? Scoresby comments on how strongly it struck him that even though there were no real grounds for the suspicion of a mutiny being planned by the passengers or crew, nobody on board seems to have had any suspicion that there was something seriously wrong with Stewart.

For the general public, the problem lay in the fact that Stewart did not act like a madman. It was widely reported that he looked and acted like a sane person, and was able to discuss the events on board the *Mary Russell* quite rationally. If Captain Stewart had conformed more closely to the accepted idea of a madman — the kind of lunatics that people went to visit for amusement in London's Bedlam Asylum (96,000 people in 1814, its last year in Moorfields), who gibbered unintelligible rubbish, pulled their hair out and engaged in hand-to-hand fights and sexual activity — then people would not have been so puzzled. But because Captain Stewart sat at his desk and wrote a well-reasoned letter to his uncle, and appeared to be quite normal, there was widespread scepticism at the inquest's verdict that he had been mad when he had murdered seven men. Mad today, sane tomorrow? It did not make sense, and looked very much like a defence of convenience, a handy subterfuge for escaping the hangman's noose.

17

The Bigger Picture

On 24 June 1828, as the *Mary Russell* was being sailed towards Cove by three men of the *Mary Stubbs*, the three apprentice boys and Captain Stewart, momentous events that were to change the course of history were taking place. On 24 June 1828, Daniel O'Connell (who was, coincidentally, an exact contemporary of Captain Stewart, also born in 1775) announced his candidacy in the Clare by-election. If O'Connell won, he would be unable to take his seat in the House of Commons until the law requiring MPs to take an anti-Catholic oath was repealed. The oath in question stated 'That the sacrifice of the Mass, and the invocation of the Blessed Virgin Mary and other saints, as now practiced [*sic*] in the Church of Rome are impious and idolatrous'.

After the great efforts made by the Ecumenical movement in the late twentieth century to emphasise the similarities between followers of Christianity, it is hard to imagine the differences that existed in the 1820s between Protestants and Catholics. Those who followed the reformed religion (the Established Church) believed that they had made a progressive decision to return to the origins of Christianity, and cast off customs and superstitions that had accumulated down the ages. The oath quoted above originates in the 39 Articles of Religion agreed in London in 1562, and approved by the Synod in Dublin in 1634. The belief in transubstantiation, the Latin Mass, and the custom of praying to the Blessed Virgin Mary and the saints were among the observances rejected by the reforms. Catholics were still considered likely to be disloyal to the Crown, and the British government was wary of Catholics in Ireland because they were the majority, forming about 85 per cent of the population. The uprisings of 1798 against British rule in Ireland were still a recent memory. Followers of the Catholic religion were harshly penalised by the status quo, being excluded from all professions for most of the eighteenth century until the restrictions were eased in 1791, and the army, navy, universities, and most importantly, the judiciary, were opened to Catholics. Hence, in 1794, the Catholic Daniel O'Connell, who had been educated abroad at Douai in France, was able to be admitted to Lincoln's Inn, London in 1794,

199

transferring two years later to Dublin's King's Inns, and called to the Irish bar in 1798, one of the first generation of Catholic Irish barristers. However, Catholics were still barred from taking seats in Parliament as they could not swear the anti-Catholic oath.

Religious differences were a favourite topic of conversation during the 1820s, and debates on theological matters attracted large crowds, and could go on for days. The *Cork Constitution* used the following joke as a space-filler on Saturday 2 August 1828:

> You will be damned, said a Roman Catholic Priest to an English sailor, if you do not embrace the tenets of my Church, and submit your conscience to her rule. 'I'm badly off then,' said the jolly tar, 'for I'll be damned if I do'.

In the 1730s when the Catholic religion was outlawed, there were some conversions to Protestantism, usually in order to hold on to the title to land. Catholic priests were actively persecuted, and wealthy Catholics often opted to be educated abroad; many had family connections in the Catholic armies of Europe following the exodus of Catholic leaders after the Treaty of Limerick in 1691. Church reorganisation following the penal years was a slow and cumbersome business, and tolerance of Catholic activity was often dependent on the attitude of the local landowner. Catholics only started building churches, in a modest way, in the late eighteenth century. All the large Catholic churches in Ireland were built after Emancipation, including those in Cork city.

Daniel O'Connell, lawyer and orator, had been intensifying his campaign for Catholic Emancipation since January 1828, when a conservative government, led by the Duke of Wellington, who was firmly anti-Emancipation, with the like-minded Sir Robert Peel as Home Secretary, took office. O'Connell stood in a by-election in County Clare in 1828 against the sitting MP, William Vesey-Fitzgerald. This constituted a challenge to the very foundation of the Protestant ascendancy, by challenging the status quo which decreed that only Protestants could become Members of Parliament. He would not be able to take his seat if he won, but he would have made clear the strength of support for his cause, and believed, correctly as it turned out, that a Catholic winning a seat would force the government to change the law requiring the oath, rather than run the risk of another Irish rebellion. Only 'forty-shilling freeholders', that is to say relatively wealthy landlords, whether Catholic or Protestant, were entitled to vote. These freeholders had been enfranchised since 1793, and over 100,000 of them were Catholics. This is an extract from the electoral manifesto entitled 'Councillor O'Connell's Grand Address to the Freeholders of County Clare':

Fellow Country men — Your county wants a Representative — I respectfully solicit your suffrages to raise me to that station.

It is true that as a Catholic, I cannot, and of course never will take the oaths at present prescribed to Members of Parliament, but the authority which created these oaths, the Parliament, can abrogate them, and I entertain a confident hope that if you elect me, the most bigoted of our enemies will see the necessity of removing from the chosen representative of the people an obstacle which would prevent him from doing his duty to his King and his Country.

The oath at present required by law is 'That the sacrifice of the Mass and the Invocation of the blessed Virgin Mary and other Saints, as now practiced in the Church of Rome, are impious and idolatrous'. Of course I never will stain my soul with such an oath; I leave that to my honourable opponent, Mr Vesey-Fitzgerald.

He has often taken that horrible oath; he is ready to take if again and asks your votes to enable him so to swear. I would rather be torn limb from limb than take it. Electors of the County Clare, choose between me, who abominates the oath, and Mr Vesey-Fitzgerald, who has sworn it full twenty times! [the address is quoted in full at http://multitext.ucc.ie/d/Oconnells_Election_Address_1828]

On Saturday 28 June, the day after the inquest was concluded at the Cork Bridewell, at about 3.15 p.m., O'Connell set out from the Four Courts in Dublin for Ennis, County Clare. The event was reported in *The Times* of London on 2 July. News of his departure spread around the Law Library, and court-rooms were emptied as barristers and jurors joined the large crowd of well-wishers that had gathered to cheer O'Connell on. He wore an elaborate green uniform, and the coach-men were also wearing green, while the coach was covered in green decorations. He acknowledged his well-wishers by raising his hat as the carriage departed, and ignored the few opponents who had gathered to hiss in disapproval. O'Connell was expected, and bonfires were lit to greet him all along the road to Clare.

On 5 July 1828, the day that William

Scoresby and Captain Hoare RN visited Captain Stewart in Cork County Gaol, Daniel O'Connell won the Clare by-election by 2,057 votes to 982. Home Secretary Robert Peel described this as 'an avalanche'. Under-Secretary Gregory, a staunch opponent of Catholic Emancipation, wrote from Dublin Castle on 7 July, 'whatever fears may be entertained from the excited feelings of the Catholics, I apprehend greater danger from the sullen indignation of the Protestants'. King George IV agreed with this sentiment. King George, Prince Regent since 1811, builder of the Royal Pavilion in Brighton, gave his name to 'the Regency', a period of distinctive architectural and artistic style and dress; he had secretly married a Catholic, Maria Fitzherbert, in 1785, a fact which he consistently denied, as it would have cost him his right to the throne. This did not stop him being in principle opposed to Catholic Emancipation. However, after O'Connell's victory, he recognised it as inevitable, the alternative being the threat of civil unrest in Ireland, always a dangerous prospect.

On 12 August 1828, the day of Captain Stewart's murder trial at Cork Assizes, according to the website cited above,

George Dawson MP for Londonderry, was

heckled by a hostile crowd during his speech at the annual Orange dinner held to commemorate the lifting of the Siege of Derry (1689). Previously an unbending defender of the Protestant Ascendancy, he now believed that the only alternative to crushing the Catholic Association was to 'look at the question with an intention to settle it'. News of Dawson's speech soon reached London. Peel was furious and reported to Wellington that 'The King has a deeper *tinge* of Protestantism than when you last saw him'. In January 1829, Peel wrote to Under-Secretary Gregory in Dublin Castle arguing that Catholic Emancipation seemed the only practicable course to take.

After much indecision, King George IV consented to the measure. The British Parliament passed the Roman Catholic Relief Bill in April 1829. George IV's final comment on the matter was that Daniel O'Connell was now the King of Ireland.

Part Three

The Trial

18

The Arraignment

Captain Stewart spent the weeks between the inquest and his formal arraignment for trial helping his legal team to prepare his defence. The jury at the inquest had concluded on 28 June, 'That several sailors and passengers were killed by the hands of Captain Stewart, being then and for some days before, in a state of mental derangement'. Because the crime had been committed 'on the High Seas' the trial came under the jurisdiction of the Court of Admiralty, which required the case to be heard before the Judges of Assize in the county or district where the vessel arrived. This meant that Captain Stewart would have to wait for the next biannual sitting of the Court of Assize, which was scheduled for early August. He had been in the Cork County Gaol since 31 June under a county magistrate's warrant issued in Skibbereen. He was suspicious of his fellow inmates, a remnant perhaps of the free-floating paranoia that had made him jump ship, and the governor let him have a cell to himself. This was probably also done for his own safety: the inmates could well have been hostile towards a man who had killed seven people, or quite simply frightened of being in his presence.

In fact, prison was probably the safest place for him at the time. Consider that it had been publicly declared by a jury that he had killed seven men. Each of these seven men had family or friends in the Cork area. Imagine that one of these men was your son, your brother, your husband or simply your friend and neighbour. He had been restrained most cruelly, tied up for over twenty-four hours and then bludgeoned to death, even though innocent of any crime. And the man who did this to seven people, instead of being unceremoniously hanged after a brief court martial, as would have been the fate of the mutineers had the mutiny really existed, was living safely in Cork County Gaol. The public sense of outrage was immense. There was widespread suspicion that the plea of insanity was a ruse to evade hanging, concocted after the event, especially in view of Captain Stewart's jumping overboard from the *Mary Stubbs* and his seeking refuge in a fishing cutter, which was seen as an attempt to escape justice. No wonder the prison authorities complained that their ability to do their job was being hampered by crowds of onlookers, hanging around outside the massive gates, hoping for a glimpse of the monstrous sea captain, or even a chance to seize the man and impose the sentence so many believed he deserved without further formality.

That the authorities were aware of the public's hostility is confirmed by the fact that when the day finally came for Captain Stewart to travel half a mile to the courthouse for his formal arraignment, his coach was assigned an escort of armed dragoons. In 1828 the courthouse was situated in the building known as the King's Old Castle in North Main Street, south of the corner with Castle Street (renamed the Queen's Old Castle after Queen Victoria's visit). The coach and its armed escort only had to leave the gates of the gaol, cross the little stone bridge over the north channel of the River Lee, turn right, and proceed up the Western Road and along Lancaster Quay and down Great George's Street (now Washington Street) into the city centre.

An arraignment is a criminal proceeding at which the defendant is called before an appropriate court, informed of the offence with which he is being charged, and asked to enter a plea of guilty or not guilty. The

211

Coroner's verdict raised some doubt as to the legality of trying Captain Stewart on a charge of murder, as it declared him to be 'in a state of mental derangement' at the time the murders were committed. A person in a state of mental derangement cannot be found guilty of murder, because they are not considered responsible for their actions. A lengthy deliberation of the City Grand Jury, which assembled at Cork on Monday 4 August 1828 decided that the prisoner could after all be charged with the murders. Because there were witnesses, who all agreed that Stewart had killed the men on board the *Mary Russell*, which he did not deny, the question to be decided by his trial was not whether he had killed the men, but whether he had been in a state of derangement at the time of the killings. Bills were accordingly prepared against Captain Stewart.

On Friday 8 August, the law lord Baron Pennefather directed that the bills should be sent up to the Grand Jury. The mate Smith, the seaman Howes and the boys Deaves and Scully were sworn in to give evidence before the Grand Jury, and were carefully examined for several hours. Then the jury returned a true bill against Captain Stewart for the capital charge (murder). Baron Pennefather then directed that the prisoner be brought to court to plead, and the Crown Solicitor was despatched by the Chief Baron to request his presence as soon as possible in court. The Chief Baron stated that he would be in attendance at six o'clock. In the meantime, Sheriff Evory proceeded to the county gaol, and returned with the prisoner in custody, in a coach with a strong guard of the 1st Dragoons. Stewart was accompanied by Mr Welsh, the governor of the gaol, and Mr John Bennett, his solicitor. This was Stewart's first appearance in public since his arrest. Word had got out that the captain of the *Mary Russell* was to appear in court and be charged. According to *The Mercantile Chronicle* (Cork, 11 August), 'the Court and all the avenues to it became crowded to excess'. The paper went on to describe the prisoner:

He is a man about five foot six inches in height, rather stout-made, of sandy complexion and hair; his eyes rather sunk in his head, and his face much florid — but he did not appear in the least dismayed. He was dressed in a black coat, white cravat and waistcoat, blue pantaloons and shoes. As he stood in the dock, his Solicitor, Mr. John Bennett to his right and the Governor of the Gaol, Mr. Welsh to his left, he lent

213

on his left elbow with his ear turned toward his council leaning to the right. Captain Stewart was then directed to hold up his right hand in order to take the oath, which he did but only partially. Mr. Welsh, the Governor put his hand under the prisoner's arm and raised it. The indictment was then read at length by the Clerk of the Crown charging him with the murder of James Goold Raynes, and the others on board the *Mary Russell*, on the high seas, one hundred leagues off the land at Baltimore. Mr. Jones then enquired if the prisoner was guilty of the felony and murder.

Mr. Bennett: Not Guilty

Chief Baron: Is he ready for trial?

Mr. Bennet (in a solemn tone): No my Lords, but he will be ready any day after tomorrow the Court may direct.

Chief Baron: Let him then be prepared on Monday morning at half past nine o'clock precisely, at which time the trial shall be entered on.

Mr. Bennett: Very well my Lords, we shall be ready.

Captain Stewart was then removed from the bar.

During this proceeding a solemn stillness prevailed throughout the whole Court, and all eyes were fixed on the wretched man, who returned again to the Gaol in the same manner as he came, with the Sheriff, a strong guard of the 1st Dragoons, and in the midst of the gaze of anxious crowds that lined the streets.

This was a pre-ordained formality (Stewart, his solicitor, the governor and the outriding dragoons would have been awaiting the summons), though also a necessary part of the legal process.

The twice-yearly Assizes, when those lawyers who were assigned to the Munster Circuit, along with their servants and clerks, travelled down from Dublin by coach, and took up residence in Cork was an eagerly awaited event, bringing an air of excitement to the city. The lawyers and their retinue stayed at designated lodgings (a security measure, so they would not have to mix with the general public, as they would in a hotel), from where they proceeded ceremoniously to the court house. Maurice Healy (1888–1943), lawyer and author of *The Old Munster Circuit* (1939), remembers as a child witnessing the event in Cork in 1893, which would not have differed much from that of 1828:

Long before I ever entered a court I was familiar with the procession of the Judges

215

from their lodgings to the Courthouse: an occasion for some little display . . . First came a trumpeter and a mounted policeman riding abreast, then two policemen, then two troopers; then came the Judges' carriage, with the military officer riding at one door and the police officer at the other; then two more troopers, followed by two more mounted police. The bravado of the street-boys sometimes occasion an 'incident' as the escort had no hesitation about using the flat of their sabres; but on the whole the proceedings were accepted by the crowd as a condescension on the part of the Government for their amusement. Within my own memory there never was any attempt to attack a judge, although in earlier days some members of the Bench had narrow escapes.

Lord Chief Justice O'Grady and Baron Pennefather were the Commissioners appointed by the Admiralty Court to hear Captain Stewart's case. Lord Chief Justice O'Grady was Standish O'Grady, first Viscount Guillamore (1766–1840), born in Mount Prospect, Limerick, the eldest son of the high sheriff Darby O'Grady. He graduated with a BA from Trinity College, Dublin, in 1784, was called to the bar at King's Inns, Dublin, in 1787 and joined the

Munster Circuit. In 1803 he became Attorney General and was one of the prosecuting counsel at the trial of Robert Emmet. He was made Lord Chief Baron in 1805. His contemporaries considered him a sound judge, and one of them called him 'the ablest man whose mind I ever saw at work.' He was famous for his wit, and praised for his knowledge of procedure. (Standish O'Grady (1846–1928), a leading figure in the Irish literary revival, was from another branch of the family, and was first cousin to Justice O'Grady's grandson, Standish, third Viscount (1832–1860).)

Richard Pennefather (1772–1859) was born in Knockevan, County Tipperary, the eldest son of Major William Pennefather, MP for Cashel. He was educated at Portarlington and Clonmel. He graduated BA from Trinity College in 1794, after a distinguished career there, and entered Middle Temple in London. He was called to the Irish bar in 1795. He appears as a King's Counsel in 1816, and in 1821 he was appointed a Baron of the Irish exchequer court and sat on the bench for thirty-eight years. *The Oxford Dictionary of National Biography* describes him as 'a sound, able and honourable judge, skilled in the digestion and elucidation of evidence, courteous in his bearing and in criminal cases lenient'. He lost his sight in his early eighties, and suggestions in the House of Commons that he be removed from the bench were opposed by admirers from both Conservative and Liberal parties, who praised his unusual judicial gifts and his continuing popularity. He retired of his own accord in 1859, and died suddenly shortly afterwards.

The chief lawyer for the prosecution, Mr Sergeant Thomas Goold (1766–1846), was born to a wealthy Protestant family in Cork. He graduated from Trinity College in 1786, and was called to the bar in 1791. His inheritance of £10,000, a huge sum in those days, was largely spent on travelling and on entertaining his friends, before he began to practise at the bar. These friends included Henry Grattan, Charles Kendal Bushe and others who opposed the Act of Union and subsequently became advocates of Catholic Emancipation, a radical stance for Protestant lawyers to adopt. It is believed that his Liberal politics hindered his legal career. He was appointed Third Sergeant in 1823, King's Sergeant in 1830, and a Master in Chancery in 1832. He was one of the greatest wits of his time at the bar, and was highly esteemed for his court work with juries, described in his day as 'the best *nisi prius* lawyer at Irish bar'. Sergeant Goold's daughter Caroline married Robert

Gore-Booth of Lissadell House, Sligo, which is where he died. She was, therefore, the grandmother of Constance Markiewicz (née Gore-Booth).

Goold had three King's Counsels (senior barristers) on his team, the Honourable Mr Plunkett, KC, Mr Quin, KC and Mr Bennett, KC. The friends of the deceased Captain Raynes had also retained a Mr O'Connell, that is to say, Daniel O'Connell, the recently elected member for East Clare, but according to the *Constitution* 'he did not give his presence during the day'. The defence team consisted of Messrs O'Loughlin, Freeman, Pigott, Croke and S. Barrington along with solicitor Mr J. Bennett.

19

The Case for the Prosecution

Sometime between the arraignment and the day of the trial, Captain Stewart was moved from the county gaol to Cork City Gaol. In spite of its formidable fortresslike stone building on a hill above Sunday's Well, north of the River Lee, the city gaol, like the county gaol, was run on benevolent principles by an enlightened governor. Captain Stewart was given sole use of an empty ward, as he had developed a fear of attack by other prisoners, a fear that in this case, unlike aboard his ship, was probably justified.

The case of the ship of seven murders had been a topic of constant, often heated debate ever since the ship's arrival in Cove on 26 June. Interest was running high, and the number of people wishing to attend the trial far exceeded the available seating. For some days before the event, the city sheriffs had been under pressure from 'persons of distinction' to obtain a place in court: in other words, anyone with any influence was using it to try and secure a place at the trial.

On the morning itself, what the newspapers described as 'a large crowd of respectable people' (all male: ladies did not attend trials) had assembled outside the courthouse before daybreak. By eight o'clock, two hours before the case was due to open, the crowd was immense. At nine o'clock those with professional roles and those engaged in the case were allowed to enter. The *Constitution*'s report continues:

Order and regularity were fully maintained, and the greatest facilities were given up to ten o'clock when the Lord Chief Baron and Baron Pennefather entered the court, at which time we recognised, near their Lordships, Major General Sir George Bingham, Colonel Turner, and several other officers — the High Sheriff of the County, and most of the gentlemen who composed the Grand Jury, also nearly all the members of the City Grand Jury, who occupied their gallery.

When all their Lordships had taken their seats, and before the case was gone into, the doors were thrown open and the courtroom was immediately packed. Outside the crush of spectators was immense and it became impossible to pass through any of the streets in the avenues of the

221

Court, and the greatest possible anxiety seemed to prevail amongst all classes and descriptions of persons.

The prisoner then appeared, dressed as before 'in a black coat with white waistcoat and cravat. His face appeared fresh and healthy, and his features exhibited composure and firmness.' (*Southern Reporter*). The Clerk of the Court, Mr Jones, ensured that Captain Stewart fully understood the consequences of the trial: that he was on trial for his life.

The first matter to be dealt with was the selection of a jury. Captain Stewart was informed that he had the privilege of challenging up to twenty members of the proposed jury, and as many more as he could show reasonable ground for objecting to. Several men were challenged on Captain Stewart's behalf by his solicitor, and several more by the Crown Solicitor.

Among those left, Mr Charles Sugrue, upon being handed the book [the Bible to swear on] objected to serving on the Jury because he was acquainted with all the circumstances of the case, and had formed an opinion which he feared was unalterable. The Lord Chief Baron said that this objection was entirely inadmissable. Any opinion that he had formed hitherto on the subject, was founded on newspaper publications, or Coffee-house conversation. He was now called upon to give a verdict on the evidence. (*Southern Reporter*).

Sugrue was spared jury duty, however, as Mr Bennett, the prisoner's solicitor, challenged him because of his 'conscientious scruples'. Another man objected because 'he had been engaged in making a collection for the benefit of the families of the sufferers, and had formed an opinion so decided that he had not hestitated to express it in different places'. Again the Lord Chief Baron said the juror could not have formed an opinion on the evidence, which he had not heard, and that was what he was called on to do now. 'The Court could never excuse the attendance of a juror on such ground.' Once again, the reluctant juror was challenged on behalf of the prisoner, and excused duty.

After about an hour, a jury of twelve good men and true were sworn in: James Leahy (foreman), Robert Honan, Thomas Lyons, George Shaw, Frederick Hall, William Power, James Boyce Foot, John Bennett, Michael O'Brien, Michael Barry, William Ridings and Thomas Rochfort. The indictment against

Captain Stewart was then read:

That he being on the high seas, about 100 leagues off the land, on Sunday, 22 June last, did with a crow bar, kill and murder James Goold Raynes, by giving him several strokes of it on his head, from which he died.

Mr Sergeant Goold then rose to address the jury. He spoke in a low tone, ensuring complete attention and silence from the packed courthouse on this hot summer's day:

My Lords and Gentlemen of the Jury, in this case I will briefly state the few facts connected with it, and advert to the points of law which may occur during the trial. The unfortunate gentleman at the bar, stands charged with the wilful murder of Captain James Raynes.

He then outlined the bare facts of the case, without going into the detail that would be produced in evidence by the survivors. His account ends with a summary:

These were the facts that furnished as lamentable history as ever were told, and as far as I can be informed or acquainted, they exceed anything in the annals of romance. Why he murdered these seven human beings is for the prisoner to say. If there existed a mutiny, the case could have been, and was now brought before a competent Judge who would ascertain that fact. If the act were done in a deranged state of mind, which for the honour of human nature, I hope was the case, the law furnishes excuses why he should not suffer its extreme penalty. It is needless for me, to draw the attention of the Bench to cases in books, on this subject, but in order to make a defence, the prisoner must state that he was deprived of his reason at the time, that he did not apprehend the consequences of his own acts and he was incapable of distinguishing between right and wrong. I will not advert to the case of Bellingham [reference cannot be traced], or the cases on record, and others, where the parties have been sent into mad-houses, and before Commissions of Lunacy, but to offer a plea of Insanity, the Jury must be satisfied that the Prisoner was not capable to distinguish between right and wrong. We shall examine all the survivors, gentlemen; and it is our wish, as indeed it is the duty of the Crown, by whom this prosecution is undertaken, to put forward every thing that can be considered favourable to the prisoner, as well as every material fact connected with the transaction. And I pray to God, for the sake of human nature, that it will appear that the prisoner is innocent; and that you by your conscientous verdict, will relieve him, and relieve our country, from the imputation which this horrible transaction, more horrible than fancy could have created, has thrown on it. I have now laid the circumstances of this deep tragedy before you. The Crown has no other object in the prosecution, than to relieve the country from so foul a stain, and from those dreadful crimes that fancy could scarcely imagine greater.

The crowd in the courtroom did not make a solitary sound as they listened to the learned Sergeant's address; indeed the prisoner never moved or displayed any form of emotion other than a flush. This may have been attributable to the temperature of the packed courthouse, as opposed to any change in his emotional state.

The Lord Chief Baron then addressed the jury, asking them to dismiss from their minds any opinions that they had already formed on the case, and all that they had read and heard about it to date. They were to be guided solely by what they heard in evidence. He suggested they might consider taking notes as it was likely to be a protraced case.

The first witness for the prosecution was Daniel Scully, aged fourteen, one of the ship's three apprentices. His evidence was much the same as he gave at the Coroner's inquest, already described, and has, along with the evidence of Smith and Howes that followed, already been used to reconstruct the account of events on board the *Mary Russell* on her passage from Barbados to Cork. Scully's evidence was followed by the mate William Smith and seaman John Howes. The boy, Richards, was in Cork Bridewell awaiting a summons to court. Daniel Scully named him as the boy who had struck Howes three times with an axe. But Howes was careful in his evidence not to name the boy who struck him three blows on the head, and apparently had no intention of pursuing the matter. Howes made it very clear that he lay no blame on the boys, who were being threatened and bullied by their captain.

The excitement in the courtroom at finally hearing a first-hand version of events from the mouths of the survivors, far more detailed than that given at the inquest, must have been intense. For example, young Daniel Scully, having denied that there was ever any intention of mutiny on board the ship, nevertheless admitted to signing a paper at the request of Captain Stewart saying that there had been a mutiny. In reply to a question from a juror, it was revealed that at the time the boy signed the paper stating there had been a mutiny on board, Captain Stewart had a pair of loaded pistols in his pocket, and promised the witness a hundred guineas on their safe return to Cove.

After the survivors, Captain Robert Callendar of the *Mary Stubbs* from New Brunswick was called to give evidence. He had sailed for Belfast after giving evidence on the first day of the inquest, 26 June, and must have returned to Cork specifically to testify at Captain Stewart's trial. His evidence was important, as he was not part of the ship's company on the *Mary Russell*, and could be relied on to have a more objective view of the circumstances on board. His was perhaps the most dramatic evidence of all, and caused a great sensation in court. Captain Callendar left Barbados one day after the *Mary Russell*, heading for Belfast (and they would therefore have followed roughly the same course across the Atlantic until making an Irish landfall). On the morning of Monday 23 June, as he was going to breakfast, a member of his crew spotted a vessel on the same course with someone on board trying for soundings (i.e. testing the depth of the water). Callendar said that was a ridiculous thing to be doing (because they were so far out at sea).

He hailed the vessel three times, on the third time was answered by a man out of the cabin window with a bottle in his hand; this was the prisoner whom witness knew in the West Indies. He called, 'for God sake to assist him as there was a mutiny on board.' Prisoner then asked him if he knew Captain Raynes and Howes. He (witness) replied he did; prisoner then said, 'They are all dead, except one man who made his escape, who was very resolute.' When he came on board, prisoner shook hands with him and gave him a loaded pistol, there was a signal of distress up when the *Mary Russell* was met; prisoner went and broke a pane with his foot in one place, and then in another and bid witness look down at the dead people; witness went down two steps of the cabin ladder and looked into the cabin. Prisoner said 'I can trample over those like dead sheep; was I not a valiant little fellow to kill so many men?' (This caused great sensation in the court).

(*Constitution*, 12 August 1828)

229

More significant for establishing Captain Stewart's state of mind was the following cross-examination of Callendar by Mr Freeman for the defence:

[The witness Callendar] knew him [the prisoner] in the West Indies; scarce knew him when he boarded, he was so much changed. He was reduced and disfigured — his eyes had not the clear white appearance they had before — said that he was without sleep for 47 days and nights, the boys said he was only 27 days without rest . . . Although the two vessels were tied together at Barbados, prisoner did not recognise the other until told of it by Hammond. When he saw Smith and Howes [on board the *Mary Stubbs*] he went down for a knife to defend himself. When he came on board the *Mary Stubbs* thinks he was not in his senses. He made several attempts to take the paper [signed by the three boys confirming mutiny] out of his breast and could not do it. He seemed to have a prevailing fear of the men rising against him . . . he seemed to triumph and exult in what he did.

Baron Pennefather requested one last piece of information from Callendar regarding

Stewart's emotional state when he jumped overboard a second time. Callendar replied 'He did not seem to make any effort to swim when he went overboard; he was wild when they first met, but wilder still when he saw the men who escaped [Smith and Howes].'

After Captain Callendar's evidence ended, William Delany, one of his seamen who helped to sail the *Mary Russell* into Cork, described Captain Stewart's second attempt to jump overboard, and how he was 'swmming on his back very well' when they caught up with him in the boat, which was, conveniently, still tied to the ship's stern. Mr Thomas Harvey of Cork gave evidence as to the value of the cargo of the *Mary Russell* — a very respectable £4,000, exclusive of King's Duty, consisting of 150 hogsheads and 59 tierces of sugar, and a quantity of leather. He concluded, saying that 'The vessel was worth £1,500. She is built about six years. The prisoner is of good character and was rather a favourite with his owners.' (In fact, according to *Lloyd's Register of Ships*, the *Mary Russell* was built in 1817.)

Smith, Scully and Callendar were all recalled and cross-examined about the statements of mutiny, and people's admission that they were involved in it. They were examined by the Chief Baron, and answered as follows:

William Smith: I did not say in Captain Callendar's presence that the men were guilty and sorry for it; what I meant to say was that I heard Captain Raynes say that he was sorry for it, alluding to his being sorry for troubling the Captain by having at all come on board.

Daniel Scully: I remember when Captain Callendar came on board the *Mary Russell*, and when he discovered Smith; during a conversation Smith did not say he was guilty [of mutiny], or that the men were guilty; when the boys were brought forward they said the men had confessed their guilt, but that they were forced to it by Captain Stewart, by the same threats he used in inducing me to sign the paper.

Captain Callendar: When I discovered Smith he did not say the men were guilty; he merely said what the boys confessed, that they all [meaning the murdered men] were guilty. I questioned Scully as to the paper he signed, and he told me that he was compelled to do so by Captain Stewart under peril of his life, but that he never

232

heard of or saw the smallest symptom of mutiny on board.

The apprentice John Deaves was the final witness for the prosecution. At this stage the court decided against any further examinations, as so far all the evidence testified to the same story.

20

The Case for the Defence

The Defence took the floor, and called a series of medical witnesses. St John Clarke Esq., MD of Skibbereen, saw the prisoner two or three times on the Sunday after he surrendered. The Chief Baron interrputed to say that an examination concerning incidents that occurred after the homicide was no use to him, and was only causing delay to the court. However, he allowed the witness to resume. Dr Clarke stated that when he saw the prisoner, he told him the entire story in a most incoherent manner, and that his face and appearance indicated insanity. Cross-examined by Sergeant Goold, Clarke admitted that he had seen the prisoner some years ago, and had not much practice in cases of madness, drawing his inference from Stewart's appeareance, manner and incoherence.

The Chief Baron interjected in a formidable tone: 'Pray, Sir, did you ever see a man after committing a homicide on seven of his fellow creatures, and can you take upon yourself to say what sort of a countenance he had?'

To which the witness could only reply, 'I could not, my Lord.'

'You may go down, Sir,' said the Chief Baron. And so ended the testimony of Dr Clarke.

Next the defence produced Edward Townsend, Esq., MD, a local Inspector of the County Gaol, examined by Mr Freeman. He explained that as a physician he had given much of his professional life to the study of insanity. His diagnosis of Captain Stewart was that he was suffering from monomania, which he explained thus:

There is one species of it [madness] called *monomania*, which means that the person afflicted might be perfectly sane on all other subjects, but a particular one. Until that cord be touched the individual might manifest cunning on many subjects. To distrust others is peculiar to every species of insanity; extreme feeling of anxiety about plots might be an attendant, also excitability and impatience.

(*Southern Reporter*, 12 August 1828)

At the mention of one symptom of insanity being impatience, the Chief Baron interrupted: 'Not the latter, I hope, Doctor,' an intervention which was greeted with loud

235

laughter in court. When this had subsided the witness continued:

Melancholy or gloominess are symptoms. The effect of a warm climate accelerates insanity on a person predisposed to it; the circumstance of a watch stopping or going might affect the person so afflicted.

Here the Chief Baron could not resist asking, in a mock-pedantic manner, intended to amuse, for clarification: 'Stopping or going, Doctor?'

Either my Lord, at times. There is a kind of madness of which a haggard or wan countenance is a symptom. I have seen the prisoner repeatedly when in the County Gaol, and consider him sane on every subject, except the one, that of a conspiracy having been formed against him; this feeling afterwards was dissipated, and though when first he came into the gaol, he required the prisoners to be searched for knives, but afterwards he got famliar with them, and that feeling gave way. On another occasion I saw him tearing some of the plastering off his cell walls, and on asking him why he did it, prisoner replied, that he saw some of the hair of a black man in it, from whom he bought rum in the West Indies, but he never after mentioned that again.

Finally Baron Pennefather asked the expert witness the question which everyone had been debating for the past six weeks:

'Can you take upon yourself to state, if the appearnce of insanity which might have marked the prisoner at the period alluded to was real or assumed?'
'I cannot, my lord, state.'
'You have had extensive conversations with him; can you from those form a notion if the insanity was genuine?'
'I cannot tell whether it was genuine or assumed, but my opinion is that it was natural. On the first day he said he should at a future period go into the history of the circumstances of what he called the mutiny. On the occasion of his detailing the story of the murder, he stopped short in the middle of it, saying 'I must write a letter to my wife'.'

To which the Chief Baron replied: 'The cord was touched there and he did not vibrate to it.'
Next Mr Piggott examined a witness for

the defence named Henry Connell. Captain Stewart's lawyers must have made great efforts in preparing for the trial to track down anyone who had evidence of past instances of madness on their client's part. Henry Connell was a brilliant find, and had an intriguing story to tell:

I recollect having taken a voyage from Gibraltar to Cork with the prisoner in May 1820; I saw no symptoms of insanity in the prisoner during the voyage out, but while we put into Baltimore in the west of this county to perform quarantine he took a suspicion against some of the people for giving information against him for smuggling; he accused me and several of the crew of having given that information; the accusation as regarded me was entirely false; there was no foundation for it; and the reason why he suspected me was, because I had been walking on deck with him for half an hour without having spoken to him. On another occasion he destroyed several pounds of tea by throwing it into a large pot, and he then said 'that he defied me'. In the course of the voyage he gave me reason to suppose him insane; those on board thought him so, and removed his pistols and razors for his own protection and theirs. He also destroyed a number of shawls, fearing that information would have been given against them as being contraband. An Officer of the 11th Regiment on board was apprehensive of danger from Stewart, and carried his pistols on board to protect himself; others of the passengers were also apprehensive of the prisoner, and fastened themselves in their cabins in dread. We were seventeen days riding quarantine.

Mr Alexander Deane, a prominent figure in the shipping industry, was the next witness for the defence, and was examined by Mr Barrington. Captain Stewart had had command of one of their vessels for many years, he said. The company had at one stage thought about sending that vessel to South America but the prisoner refused the command because he was 'afraid of going to a southern climate, on account of his head'. He added that the captain had always been thought of as a very humane man and was well liked and respected by all who sailed with him.

Another shipping agent, Simon Ring, testifed that he had known Captain Stewart for thirteen or fourteen years, and said that while the prisoner's general character was that of a humane man, he was also considered flighty, given to paying attention to dreams, and was afraid of ghosts. He believed the prisoner to be of weak intellect, and said that his wife was always in terror about him when he went to a warm climate. Another witness, James Mahony, described an incident during a voyage to Trinidad in which the captain had disagreed with his crew, and had been about to strike the mate with the lead line, until witness interfered and caught him.

The next to take the witness stand was Dr Richard Maguire, the medical attendant of the city and county gaols of Cork. He first examined Captain Stewart on the day he was committed, 1 July 1828, and had seen him nearly every day since. The first time that Dr Maguire saw him he considered him decidedly insane on the subject of this enquiry. It took a fortnight before he would mingle with the other prisoners, for he considered that they were all conspiring against him. Only when he had befriended a gaoler and under-gaoler would he believe that he was safe among the inmates. Maguire believed that the insanity was not 'affected', because the prisoner always denied being insane. He did not refuse food and drink, on the contrary, he saw him eat and drink voraciously, which strengthened his opinon of his insanity. Under cross-examination Maguire reported that he believed that the prisoner was insane on only one subject, and sane on all others. He said that the prisoner had become more rational with the passing of time.

The last witness for the defence, Dr Osborne, physician to the Cork Lunatic Asylum, was to become an important figure in Captain Stewart's life. But on this occasion his expert medical opinion was challenged on legal grounds by the Chief Baron. Under examination by Mr O'Loughlin for the defence it was revealed that Dr Osborne had never examined Captain Stewart, spoken to him in conversation, nor even laid eyes on him before that day. But having heard the evidence given that day in court, he had no doubt that the prisoner must have been insane when he committed the act. To which the Baron replied: 'Why then, you have formed yourself into a thirteenth Juror? The whole object of the trial is to ascertain the question you have answered so readily: might not he assume insanity to cover his act?' At this the court erupted in laughter. When it had died down, Dr Osborne spoke again and said, 'I only judge from the evidence given'.

Lord Chief Baron: How can you say that all the witnesses swore truly?

Dr Osborne: I presume all the witnesses swore truly as they swore upon their oaths: and my opinion was given from the experience I have had as physician at the Lunatic Asylum for the last two years, and from the attention I have given to insanity generally.

Lord Chief Baron: Do you think that every man that commits a diabolical act is mad?

Dr Osborne: Certainly not, my Lord.

Lord Chief Baron: Then, sir, how can you take it upon you to say whether the prisoner acted with an intention of screening himself from the consequences of a diabolical act which he determined to commit, or whether it was a visitation from God?

The fine distinction between a diabolical act — an act undertaken in full awareness at the instigation of the Devil — and a visitation from God — an act undertaken while deprived of normal powers of reasoning — is the hinge upon which the whole case now rested. Medical evidence was not sufficient, as it is in today's courts, to have a person declared insane: it was up to the judge and the jury, having heard the evidence, to decide if the prisoner were sane or insane. If Captain Stewart had committed a diabolical act, and killed seven men, while knowing what he was doing, then he was guilty of murder, and would hang for his crime. But if he had acted while under a visitation from God, (that is to say, while not in his right mind), he could not be held morally responsible for his crime, and would merit a verdict of not guilty, having committed the act while mentally deranged.

Dr Osborne was about to read from a piece of paper in his hand listing the symptoms of insanity, but he was stopped. The court took the view that this witness could have been valuable to listen to had the prisoner received any medical care from him, but as the court had already heard evidence from two separate doctors who did attend him, Dr Osborne's evidence had no place in court.

Mr Freeman for the defence now put it to the presiding Barons that they wished to enter the verdict of the Coroner's court into evidence, as it gave credence to the insanity of the prisoner. Baron Pennefather interjected that he did not believe that such a record could be admissible, and Baron O'Grady backed him up by saying 'If you had any case to show it was ever received, you would cite it; but you shall not make the experiment on us'. With that, the defence rested.

These are extracts from the Lord Chief Baron's summing up of the case for the jury:

Gentlemen of the Jury, I am very sorry that a great and most responsible duty has fallen upon us — perhaps I should have said, on you — for it devolves more on the Jury than on the Court in this instance, there being very little of law in the case; the whole rests upon the opinion which you shall deliberately form, upon a consideration of the evidence, as to the prisoner's state of mind at the time of this transaction. That the prisoner has been unfortunate enough to commit the act, admits of no doubt. The question therefore is whether he acted deliberately by the instigation of the Devil, or whether he acted under the visitation of God which impaired his sense. When it pleases God so to deprive a man of his understanding, it belongs not to any human tribunal to bring that man to punishment. Hence you are to consider, Gentlemen, whether the prisoner acted *malo animo* [with evil intent], or whether he acted under the visitation of God. If he did not know what he was about or was unable to distinguish right from wrong, or under a delusion of mind perpetrated the act which he in his better moments would not commit, in any of these cases it must lead to his acquittal.

The Lord Chief Baron reminded the jury of the evidence which they had heard from Henry Connell, Alexander Deane, Simon Ring and James Mahony, all of whom had given reason to suspect that there had been instances in Captain Stewart's past that had caused him to be feared and restrained. Then he continued:

The credit to be given to the evidence of those witnesses is entirely a matter for your consideration, but if you, Gentlemen of the Jury, are inclined to rely on their evidence, it will lead more to your coming to a right opinion on the case than any abstract discussions on insanity.

The question, I again repeat, is whether the prisoner acted by the instigation of the Devil, or under the visitation of God, which left him no longer master of himself at the time he committed the offence.

If on the whole case you have a rational ground for doubt, it is the duty of the Court to direct you on this as on all other occasions, to lean to the side of mercy. If on the other hand, your minds are made up as to the prisoner's guilt, you are bound to pronounce him guilty without hesitation.

It is right for me to warn you that you are not to suffer your feelings to be

245

operated on by the magnitude of the crime; the deplorable carnage which has taken place, and the enormity of the crime, is certainly, I conceive, some presumption in favour of the prisoner, and some reason why we should suppose him innocent; if he acted deliberately and by the instigation of the Devil, he is one of the most celebrated monsters who have disgraced their country, and human nature; for he has been guilty of one of the most foulest and most brutal acts which was ever committed by man, and one which must render him most obnoxious in the eyes of God. Gentlemen you will retire now and consider your verdict.

It was now a quarter to six in the evening, and the court had been sitting since 10 a.m. on a hot August day. The judges and jury left the court. The relief offered by a break must have been enormous for the legal teams and for those attending the trial. But for the jury it was the most difficult and demanding part of their day. They were only gone for about forty-five minutes when word was received that a verdict could be expected within the next half hour. At 7.10 p.m., the court reconvened, the jury reappeared and had their names read out, and the prisoner was placed at the bar. In the hushed and expectant court the foreman of the jury stood and delivered their verdict: 'Guilty, but we believe him to have been in an insane state of mind at the time.'

The Chief Baron called out to them, 'We cannot receive such a verdict; go back and rectify it.'

It fell to Baron Pennefather to explain the relevant point of law to the jury and the rest of the court: 'The verdict is actually tantamount to 'Not Guilty', for the law does not recognise that as guilt, which is committed when a person does not know right from wrong. You can amend it without leaving your box.' After a short pause, the foreman of the jury, James Leahy, handed a paper to the Clerk of the Crown who read it aloud: 'Not Guilty, because we believe that the prisoner was labouring under mental derangement when he committed the act.'

The prisoner had remained inscrutable throughout the day-long trial, not reacting to any of the evidence, not flinching at the appearance of the survivors, Smith and Howes, the apprentice Daniel Scully, nor his colleague, Captain Callendar, and not reacting to the tales of his past mental troubles as revealed by a string of witnesses. As more than one newspaper remarked, he showed no symptoms of mental or bodily weakness throughout the trial. Those who had expected to see external signs of madness in Captain Stewart were disappointed. He retained his composure throughout, looking every inch what he actually was: a respectable sea captain, used to commanding ship and crew, held in high esteem by his ship-owning employers, and in his private life, a loving husband and father. Before he was removed from the dock he expressed his gratitude to Mr Bennett, his solicitor, and to his counsel, and asked that the verdict be given to his wife immediately. Newspaper reports differ on what happened next; some say he fell to his knees immediately on hearing the verdict, raised his hands to heaven as if in prayer, and remained that way for about half a minute. Others report him making a speech after thanking his legal team but before leaving the court. This is William Scoresby's version, based on the *Southern Reporter*:

Just as he was about retiring, he lifted up his hands, and with great apparent fervour, said 'I have great reason to bless God; for if I had committed the murder wilfully, I would not have wished to live myself, but I did not!' This concluding act of the prisoner excited the attention, and seemed to awaken, in his behalf, the better feelings of the great body of the audience, producing, no doubt, in many that attended that day, a substitution of commiseration and compassion for the previous feelings of repugnance.

So according to Scoresby, the verdict of not guilty by reason of insanity allowed people to feel compassion for a man whom they had previously reviled as a mass murderer.

Captain Stewart was conveyed back to Cork City Gaol, to be kept in safe custody until further orders. His actual sentence was 'That he be kept in close confinement during life, or during his Majesty's pleasure'.

The day had a happy ending for one other participant in the events. Before the court was adjourned at half past seven, Baron Pennefather directed that the boy Henry Richards, who had been detained in the Bridewell, a short walk away from the courthouse, should be discharged. The twelve-year-old apprentice and his family must have been greatly relieved to know that no charges were to be pressed for his axe attack on John Howes.

21

Reflections on the Trial

The demand for the *Cork Constitution* was so great that a reprint of the edition carrying the trial report — 'a record of one of the most extraordinary occurrences in History, arising out of mental aberration' — was issued. The reporting of the trial was excellent, with the *Southern Reporter*, the *Cork Constitution* and the *Freeman's Journal* agreeing on all the main points. Reports in the Dublin and London papers were based on one or other of the Cork versions, presumably by some kind of licensing agreement. A pamphlet containing a full transcript of the trial was published by J. Connor of Tuckey Street in 1828.

To those accustomed to modern court procedures, it is remarkable how much evidence was heard in so short a time, and that the court sat until 7.30 p.m. in order to conclude the proceedings in one day. The fluency and high level of literacy of those giving evidence, especially the seamen and the boys is also remarkable, but it is hard to know to what extent their speech might have been 'tidied up' for publication by reporters following the conventions of the time.

The case is unusual in that both prosecution and defence are seeking the same verdict — not guilty by reason of insanity. It is surely unusual in a court of law that the prosecution should open the case by stating it as the duty of the Crown 'to put forward every thing that can be considered favourable to the prisoner'. Then Goold adds, 'I pray to God, for the sake of human nature, that it will appear that the prisoner is innocent'. A verdict of not guilty by reason of insanity would also be a good verdict for Ireland, according to Sergeant Goold's opening address: 'I pray to God, for the sake of human nature, that it will appear that the prisoner is innocent; and that you by your conscientous verdict, will relieve him, and relieve our country, from the imputation which this horrible transaction, more horrible than fancy could have created, has thrown on it.'

What is probably most remarkable of all is the definition of insanity used by the judiciary in 1828. The condition is described purely in religious terms. Remember the Chief Baron's words: 'The question, I again repeat, is whether the prisoner acted by the instigation of the Devil, or under the visitation of God, which left him no longer master of himself at the time he committed the offence.' People who do bad things are possessed by the devil, but people who are what we call mentally ill, are visited by God. That being deprived of one's normal faculties of reason should be described as a visitation of God seems strange indeed to modern ears. But in our grandparents' generation, a person with intellectual disabilities was described as being a *duine le Dia* — a person with God.

William Scoresby considers the verdict of guilty but insane in a chapter of *The Mary Russell* entitled 'The Responsibility of Maniacs'. He praises the judiciary for 'the wise and merciful principle that the unhappy being whom it has pleased the Bestower of reason [i.e. God] to deprive of his reason, is no longer amenable to any human tribunal'. But then he draws an analogy between the drunkard, who brings a temporary madness upon himself by his wilful self-indulgence, and the lunatic, who may on occasion have recklessly allowed the disease to develop 'by his own conscious indiscretion'.

For as the moral mania which results from the excessive indulgence of any passion or vice, might, under a due resistance of the cause, by Divine grace, have been prevented; so it is presumed that the mental or physical mania, to which our constitution may be liable, might, in many cases, be likewise prevented or subdued by proper personal resistance and discipline.

In other words, avoiding mental illness is a matter of vigilance and willpower. Scoresby then refers to the medical philosophy of the treatment of lunatics that prevailed at the time:

. . . the endeavour to produce quiescence of mind, along with an improved condition of body; and through an improved habit of body, to correct the excitability and aberrations of the mind. And, except in cases where a defective or permanently deranged organization of the system renders the application of this principle necessarily inefficacious, the results are generally found to be eminently successful.

So if you are prone to attacks of mania, it is your moral duty to do all you can to avoid their onset, chiefly by living a quiet, well-ordered life.

Scoresby restates his belief in Captain Stewart's innocence of 'blood-guiltiness' in the massacre he carried out, but believes Stewart could have done more to prevent the onset of mania:

If the principles herein laid down be correct, he was no doubt blameable, and that especially in a self-indulgence to which he is said to have been addicted — the taking of stimulants. It does not appear, indeed, that he drank to the extent of intoxication; but he was certainly in the habit of using ardent spirits, at different periods, daily, and in this, if aware of his excitable constitution, and predisposition to insanity, lay, it would seem, his principal blame in that melancholy voyage. He was not conscious, perhaps, of the pernicious tendency of this self-indulgence; certainly he could have no conception of 'how great a matter a little fire kindleth' (James iii, 5, 6,).

Nowadays medical opinion would not be concerned with the moral duty of a person prone to attacks of mania, though a quiet, well-ordered life is still recommended.

However, there is a core of truth in Scoresby's observation. There was no issue of grog on board the *Mary Russell*; only the captain was entitled to strong drink, which he occasionally shared with favoured shipmates. Captain Stewart was waving a bottle of snuff out of the window when the *Mary Stubbs* came alongside. While in his cell at Cork County Gaol, he is described by Dr Townsend as tearing plaster off the wall because he saw a hair of a black man who sold him rum in Barbados. Who knows what was in the snuff bottle, especially if he bought it on the docks in Barbados? And the rum sold in the West Indies was known to be far more potent than spirits available in Europe. It could well have been the case that his use of stimulants accelerated and intensified the onset of his mania.

William Saunders Hallaran (1765-1825), the founding father of Irish psychiatry, in his book *Practical Observations on the Causes and Cures of Insanity* (Cork, 1818) attributes the great increase in the numbers of insane at the turn of the century in part to 'the unrestrained use of ardent spirits'. He also subscribes to the prevailing belief that 'a hot climate tends to excite severe sensations of remorse, followed by maniacal symptoms'. Elsewhere he writes: 'It is a well-established fact that our troops in the West Indies have been known at times to encounter more danger from incautious indulgences in this way [i.e. by drinking newly distilled spirits] than from the most sanguinary conflicts with the enemy.'

Nowadays the responsibility of defining a

prisoner's mental condition rests with a consultant psychiatrist, and not with a judge or jury. This is the relevant section of the Criminal Law Insanity Act 2006 (our italics):

Where an accused person is tried for an offence and, in the case of the District Court or Special Criminal Court, the court or, in any other case, the jury finds that the accused person committed the act alleged against him or her and, *having heard evidence relating to the mental condition of the accused given by a consultant psychiatrist*, finds that

a) the accused person was suffering at the time from a mental disorder, and

b) the mental disorder was such that the accused person ought not to be held responsible for the act alleged by reason of that fact that he or she

(i) did not know the nature and quality of the act, or

(ii) did not know that what he or she was doing was wrong, or

(iii) was unable to refrain from committing the act,

the court of the jury, as the case may be, shall return a special verdict to the effect that the accused person is not guilty by reason of insanity.

Dr Brendan D. Kelly, consultant psychiatrist in the Department of Adult Psychiatry, University College Dublin, who practises at the Mater Hospital, has a special interest in the insanity defence, as it is called, and in psychiatric practice in nineteenth-century Ireland. He recently published a paper, *Criminal insanity in 19th century Ireland, Europe and the United States: Cases, contexts and controversies (International Journal of Law and Psychiatry* (32, 2009, pp 362–368)), that considered, among other issues, the insanity defence. He quotes Dr Isaac Ray (1807–1881), one of the founding fathers of forensic psychiatry in the United States, on the provenance of this defence:

In all civilised communities, ancient or modern, insanity has been regarded as exempting from punishment of crime, and under some circumstances at least, as vitiating the civil acts of those who are affected with it. The only difficulty or diversity of opinion, consists in determining who are really insane, in the meaning of the law.

The verdict 'guilty but insane' was the one traditionally used in Irish courts until The Criminal Law Insanity Act in 2006 changed the verdict to 'not guilty by reason of insanity'. In this context, Dr Kelly found the end of Captain Stewart's trial, where the Chief Baron sends back the jury to rephrase their verdict of 'guilty but insane', so that it reads 'not guilty by reason of insanity' highly significant. He explains: 'Up until the 2006 Act, the verdict 'guilty but insane' was always used. It took decades of serious campaigning by many psychiatrists to get this changed to the correct verdict, 'not guilty by reason of insanity'. So I was intrigued by the end of the trial in 1828, where the Baron just told the jury to change their verdict. Within the space of a few minutes they did something that subsequently took decades of campaigning to achieve.'

The use of the verdict 'guilty but insane' just evolved over the years, to become the common usage. The reason it needed to be changed was because it is not correct. Dr Kelly explains:

Hundreds of people have lived and died in the Central Mental Hospital having been told that they were guilty, when in fact they were not guilty by reason of insanity. This change is of really quite profound significance to a forgotten minority. If someone who is seriously mentally ill kills somebody, and they are tried, they will be sent to Dundrum Central Mental Hospital, and they will spend many years reflecting on their trial. It is only humane that they should reflect upon the words 'not guilty' rather than spend the years reflecting on the word 'guilty'. It is interesting that Captain Stewart's case prefigured the change in the law, but it took the law nearly 200 years to catch up with the Chief Baron and the jury.'

It is quite possible that Captain Stewart's reaction to being told that he was not guilty by reason of insanity — his falling to his knees, and thanking God — expressed his sense of relief. The trial told him that he was insane at the time he killed seven men. Dr Kelly comments: 'This may have brought a sense of certainty to him, a sense of relief. Many people would find it hard to believe that any human being could do what he did, kill seven men, and believe such an act was entirely right. There is a part within the minds of almost all individuals that knows such an act is in some way wrong — and this may or may not persist even if the individual is so mentally ill that they are paranoid, as in the case of Captain Stewart, to the point of jumping into the sea days after the event.'

The verdict brought a great sense of relief to Captain Stewart, allowing him to say, 'I was not myself when I did it'.

If Captain Stewart were to be tried today for the same crime, would the same verdict — not guilty by reason of insanity — have been returned? Dr Kelly has no doubt that it would. 'There is no question of diminished responsibility: he was very clearly insane when he committed the act. This would be one of those rare cases where both prosecution and defence psychiatrist would be in complete agreement: not guilty by reason of insanity.' Similarly, the prosecution and defence lawyers in Captain Stewart's case agreed that there was only one possible verdict: not guilty by reason of insanity.

The diagnosis of monomania has long been discarded, as psychiatric knowledge grew, and treatment developed. We asked Dr Kelly what his diagnosis of Captain Stewart's condition would be. His reply was: 'Overall, in terms of diagnosis, Captain Stewart would certainly be described nowadays as being psychotic, having an episode of psychosis. This can be caused by one or more things, most commonly, having schizophrenia, but also having bipolar disorder, also known as manic depression. The events on the *Mary Russell* would seem to have happened during an episode of mania with elation: he was suffering from psychotic elation in the context of bipolar disorder.'

Dr Kelly agrees with Scoresby that the various substances ingested by Captain Stewart, snuff and Barbados rum, might have been a precipitating factor: 'It emerges at the trial that there were episodes in the past, when he had acted strangely, but he had recovered, and was able to continue captaining ships, which is also typical of bipolar disorder.'

Within a psychiatric context, elation is not always a happy condition. Dr Kelly explains:

Obviously Stewart is extremely troubled. He is not happy in his elation. He was paranoid in it, and that happens quite commonly. One of the key distinguishers between elation and schizophrenia would be the presence or absence of bizarre delusions. For a captain of a ship to have a delusion that people are about to have a mutiny is not wildly bizarre. It is not a bizarre delusion of schizophrenia, but more consistent with paranoid elation in bipolar disorder.

The incident with the watch stopping and starting is a classic illustration of Captain

Stewart's delusional interpretation of events, adding a significance to events that they do not really merit. He believed that the watch had been tampered with by the boys, therefore the boys were not to be trusted. Dr Kelly comments: 'That confirms certainly that he was psychotic, that is, he had lost the ability to distinguish between objective and subjective reality. It is a classic feature of psychosis, and it is very nicely described by William Scoresby.'

Another reason for opting for the diagnosis of bipolar disorder rather than schizophrenia lies in Captain Stewart's subsequent ability to make a complete recovery: 'The bipolar element would explain why he was so normal in Cork gaol, and why he was able to keep working after the earlier episodes described at the trial. He had long periods of wellness, when he was able to captain ships and work as normal. And he had no progressive deficit, the downward steps, that sometimes occur in some people with schizophrenia. His ability to recover completely between episodes is more consistent with bipolar disorder, rather than schizophrenia.'

22

Cork City Gaol 1828 – 1830

Cork City Gaol is an imposing, fortress-like building that looks more like a castle than a purpose-built gaol. It is situated on a hill above Sunday's Well, a site chosen in the belief that it would discourage 'gaol fever'. It is built of red sandstone quarried from the hill, and is in the shape of an 'H', with the crossbar being the governor's house. It dates from 1824, and, when it opened, was described as 'the finest in the three kingdoms' (i.e. England, Ireland and Scotland). At that time it had 54 cells, accommodating 154 males, and 48 cells for 96 female prisoners. Each ward had a day room and airing yard, and in one of these was a treadmill used to pump up water to supply of the prison. There were separate places of worship for Protestants and Roman Catholics. Many of the prisoners at the time Captain Stewart was there were awaiting transportation to Australia.

Captain Stewart's wife, Betsy, and his four children were regular visitors to the city gaol during his first two years of confinement. His children, Henry (then aged ten), Francis (seven), Margaret (five) and Timothy (two) were allowed in two at a time. In 1829 Betsy brought her husband the sad news of the death of Thomas Hammond at the age of twelve. (His father, James, was Francis' godfather). Thomas had lived only one more year after being sent to Barbados to improve his health, and witnessing seven murders on the return journey.

During those early years of confinement Stewart embraced religion with great fervour, and his friendship with William Scoresby became increasingly important to him. Scoresby was a frequent visitor to Cork, as his wife had not been able to settle in Liverpool, and spent much of her time on her family's estate at Corkbegg, eventually staying there full time until her husband should find a new parish. Scoresby's biographers, Tom and Cordelia Stamp, comment: 'One is tempted to wonder if Scoresby's parishioners of the labouring poor and seamen played any part in her dissatisfaction.' Whatever the reason, his regular visits to his wife at her family home allowed Scoresby to continue his scientific observation of 'this extraordinary man'. To Scoresby's great delight, Captain Stewart had become profoundly religious during the first year of his incarceration. When Scoresby visited him in the city gaol on 18 August 1829, he reports:

> ... the miserable man, who under the influence of temporary derangement destroyed the lives of seven of his unoffending sailors, has not only escaped that violent mortal punishment which he himself inflicted on others, but has obtained, as far as human judgment, assisted by Scriptural evidences, can determine, mercy and pardon at the hands of an infinitely merciful God.

The governor of the city gaol had put Captain Stewart by himself in one of the better wards and, out of respect for Stewart's feelings, did not allow anyone into his ward without his permission. Thus he was spared the string of curious onlookers who might otherwise have queued up for a look at the man who had killed seven men, and who claimed to be mad but acted completely sane.

Captain Stewart gave the Reverend Scoresby a warm welcome, and Scoresby found him well: 'His appearance now differed from what I had formerly observed, in his complexion being less florid, the expression of his eye less sharp, his manner more subdued, and his dress, from the effects of constant wear, less respectable.'

When Scoresby arrived Stewart was busy teaching two of his children writing and arithmetic, which, along with religious instruction, was part of their daily routine. He welcomed Scoresby to his apartment, and reassured him that he remembered him well from his visits the year before.

Then he added 'I knew your father also: was he not a great ship-owner?' On my answering that he was a ship-owner he said, 'I knew him when he was fitting out the *John*, about [blank] years ago; she was a teak-built ship. Your father wished me to have gone as his mate to the whale fishery, but I had another engagement which prevented me.'

Scoresby makes no comment on this strange coincidence, and seems to have accepted it as the truth. After that, Stewart immediately began talking about his religious feelings and anxieties. Scoresby was astonished to find that a man who twelve months before had held 'very erroneous views of the principles of the Gospel' now speaking knowledgably on leading matters of Christian doctrine and showing a wide knowledge of the scriptures. He had been helped along this road by the chaplain and inspector of the gaol, Dr

Quarry. He had taken to reading twenty chapters of the scriptures daily on his knees, as well as what he read on his bed, and with his children. He commenced his lessons with them by reading the Morning Service, and he had developed the habit of reading part of the Commination Service, which he said was particularly applicable to his case. (The Commination Service is the Liturgy for Ash Wednesday, and includes the recital of divine threats against sinners. It was initially instituted for public penitents, who stood outside the church door wearing sackcloth and ashes.) Stewart quoted from Psalm LI which is used in that service, repeating with strong feeling the passages: 'Make me a clean heart, O God! And renew a right spirit within me . . . Deliver me from blood-guiltiness, O God!' Stewart concluded his children's daily lessons by reading the Evening Prayer, and spent the rest of the evening in devotional exercises. Scoresby was so astonished by this schedule that he asked the governor, the chaplain and one of the medical officers to confirm it, and they did so. Scoresby quotes Stewart on his new-found sense of religion:

I used to think that my being moral and sober, and having prayers in my ship on Sundays, was enough for my salvation; but now I see the error. All that man can do is nothing, without faith and repentance. I used to think, that because so many were worse than myself, I should have little to fear; and that God would not surely condemn such multitudes of people who were thoughtless and wicked, but spare them from his infinite mercy. But now I see that if he condemned Sodom and Gomorrah, and also the world before the flood, exactly as he had threatened, he would surely condemn every sinner that did not repent and believe the Gospel.

When asked whether he was comfortable in his present situation, Stewart assured Scoresby that he was, and that he had no desire to be released, but would rather live and die in the place he now occupied:

For I am better and safer for my soul's good where I am: if I should be released everyone would point to me, and say, There goes that miserable man who killed his sailors! If I were to go to a place of worship, people would point at me there. And (with a peculiar energy he added) I might be tempted to deny that I was the unfortunate Stewart — and I would rather die than tell a lie.

To Scoresby all this indicated not only a sound mind, but also a wise and understanding heart. It never occurs to Scoresby that Stewart might now be in the grip of a form of religious mania, which is the first thought that springs into the more sceptical 21st-century mind.

Scoresby could not resist investigating whether the 'monomania' with which Stewart had been afflicted was entirely removed. So he made the bold move of asking him a direct question: 'What are your present views respecting the unhappy transaction in the *Mary Russell*?'

Without either hesitation or apparent excitement, he replied that 'his mind on that subject had altogether changed; for he now saw that his poor fellows were innocent, and that he committed the act he had done, under the influence of derangement. He was now convinced that his mind had been wrong, from the curious visions which he fancied he saw after he came into confinement. Yet one of these visions, which he described as consisting of seven lights that appeared in his cell, had given him comfort. He fancied he perceived in it a token, that his poor fellows, being innocent, had found mercy. And this hope was his chief comfort: that God had heard their earnest prayers at the hour of death; and if so, he had then little to regret concerning them, as to what had happened would be their gain [i.e., he need not regret their deaths because, since they were innocent, they would have gone straight to Heaven].

When Scoresby asked him whether he felt to blame for what he had done, Stewart answered:

That God would pardon him, and receive him, because he had done it in ignorance; for he could appeal unto Heaven for his veracity when he said, that he did it under the strongest conviction that he was driven to it by the greatest necessity, firmly believing at the time that there was no other means in the world of saving his life.

Stewart took advantage of Scoresby's theological expertise to ask him for explanations on a number of passages of scripture that had been puzzling him. Scoresby noticed that the questions were chiefly concerned with texts on which the Roman Catholic Church held what he considered erroneous views. Stewart admitted he had probably been tainted with such errors because his wife was a papist, and he had constant dealings with members of the Roman Church. From baptismal records we know that he allowed his children to be baptised into the Catholic Church, even though their sponsors, including the ship owner, James Hammond, often came from the Established Church. Scoresby reports that 'Hence, though he [Stewart] was a Protestant, he could not help sometimes praying for the souls of his poor men: it could do no harm, he thought, and he found comfort in doing so.'

The prefatory remark 'though he was a Protestant' is puzzling to those not familiar with the tenets of the most severe form of Protestantism, which forbids praying for the souls of the dead. This is a key difference between Protestantism and Catholicism. The logic behind the prohibition is that, since Christ died to save the souls of the dead, there is no need to pray for their souls. It has nothing to do with the fact that the dead men are Catholic, but applies equally to all the souls of the dead, whatever their denomination. Also, and very importantly, the fact that Stewart finds comfort in praying for the souls of the men he killed suggests that he is finally suffering genuine remorse for his deed.

During the summer of 1829 Captain

Stewart told Scoresby about an incident in his younger days that explains the sense of guilt that haunted Stewart, and reveals the origins of his fear of Providence taking revenge on him for sins past. The story gives a flavour of the exchanges between these two seasoned seafarers, cast together in such unusual circumstances. The disgraced sea captain and the eminent scientist and pastor both obviously relished recollecting the excitement and danger of their earlier seafaring days. This is Stewart's story in full, as retold by Scoresby:

In the month of December, 1825, he was attempting to bring a small schooner, of only 80 tons burden, and five hands across the Atlantic from America, deeply laden with deals [timber]. Soon after leaving the coast, they encountered so heavy a gale as to oblige them to heave-to. The personal attendance of the crew on deck, where they were greatly exposed, being now useless, all hands, excepting one, retreated to the cabin. Providentially, the one who was left in turn to look out, had occasion to go below, when, at the very moment, the vessel was struck by a heavy sea, which threw her so completely over, that a large chest, belonging to one of the crew, was

272

pitched from the cabin floor against the coamings of the sky-light, and some papers that lay on the Captain's bed were struck up against the roof of the state-room! In this awful condition they remained but a few moments — the closeness of the hatches and sky-light, with the solid construction of the stern, preventing their being at once inundated — when the deck cargo having separated, the vessel righted. They all now rushed upon deck, terrified at the extraordinary event that had occurred. After the first alarm had subsided, two men were set to clear the wreck about the decks, whilst the rest went to some requisite duty below, when another heavy sea was shipped. This struck the mainmast, near the deck, with such violence as not only to carry it away, but to hurl, by the reaction, the head of the mast over the side to windward! It also broke all the deck beams, and washed overboard two poor fellows who were exposed to its action. One of them however, after going under the vessel's bottom, got entangled in the wreck of the mast, as he rose to windward, and was hauled safely on board. The other perished!

The vessel, after this, strained so much, that to prevent her falling to pieces, they set themselves to work to swifter the sides together with a hawser (an operation described in the account of St. Paul's tempestuous voyage towards Rome, as 'under-girding the ship'), and in this they so far succeeded as to prevent the threatened calamity. They also let go the anchor, though in deep water, allowing the cable to run out to the end by the resistance of which, the schooner's head was kept towards the sea, so as to preserve them from being overwhelmed with the waves. For six days they continued in a state of extreme peril, the gale not having subsided during the whole of that time; when, being reduced to the last extremity of suffering and despair, they descried a ship approaching them. Providentially the schooner lay directly in her track, so as to bring the two vessels within hail of each other. At no small risk of his masts and sails, the kindly stranger hauled suddenly to, and after making a tack to windward, hoisted out his long-boat. But the highly excited hopes of the little crew were almost sunk into despair, when they observed that, from the heavy sea that was still running, the boat filled alongside. The persevering benevolence of the Captain, however, prevailed over this discouragement. With very masterly address, he recovered his boat, and having again beaten up to the foundering schooner, suddenly dropped it into the sea, secured by a hawser, and passed it clear astern. It was then manned over the stern, and speedily came within reach of the anxious little party, all of whom were thus rescued from their desperate condition. In remarking upon this extraordinary deliverance, Captain Stewart observed 'that he ascribed his subsequent misfortunes to his neglect of this providential warning, and to the breaking of the vows which he then made. He had vowed before God, in his extremity of despair, that if He would this time spare him, he would live to his service and glory. But when safety was attained, he soon forgot his vows, and therefore a worse thing came upon him!

It is a rousing tale of adventure and camaraderie, and an excellent illustration of the modern seafaring saying 'There's no such thing as an atheist in a storm'. But could the story also be a cunning ruse by Stewart, to flatter his distinguished visitor, who had indeed retired from the sea and devoted himself to God? Scoresby had done the very thing that Stewart had not done. In a way that seems decidedly superstitious (Stewart's consistent weakness), Stewart was now blaming his subsequent misfortunes on his failure to keep the vows he made in the storm.

23

Asylum 1830 – 1873

In the summer of 1830, Scoresby was back in Cork again, and was told that Stewart had been removed to Cork Lunatic Asylum where he had been 'in a state of violent derangement'. The Cork Lunatic Asylum was opened in 1789, in what is now Cork's South Infirmary, under physician William Saunders Hallaran, the author of *Practical Observations on the Causes and Cure of Insanity*, cited above. Dr Hallaran was a humane and enlightened thinker, as is evident in his opening line, 'The cloud of darkness and uncertainty which still, unfortunately, pervades this department of medical science is deeply to be lamented'. He considers both the mental and the bodily causes of insanity, and re-evaluates traditional treatments such as bleeding, emetics and purgatives, and remedies like digitalis (very useful in the treatment of mania), opium, camphor and mercury. He believed, unlike most of his contemporaries, that in many cases mental derangement was curable. Physical treatments recommended for the

277

long-term mentally ill included fresh air, exercise, hot baths or shower baths, and a light diet featuring fresh vegetables and plenty of starch, with meat three times a week when the budget allowed. The asylum attempted to provide appropriate occupation for the recovering lunatic, usually gardening and food preparation, but whatever suited the inmate would be encouraged, as was the case with the artist mentioned below, who sketched Captain Stewart in his mania, and eventually made a full recovery. A recent academic paper by Dr Brendan D. Kelly, *Dr William Saunders Hallaran and Psychiatric Practice in 19th-century Ireland*, concludes that many aspects of Hallaran's progressive approach to psychiatric care remain relevant today (*Irish Journal of Medical Science, 2008, Vol. 177, 1, pp 79–84*). Dr Hallaran had died two years before Captain Stewart was transferred to the asylum, but the institution continued to be run according to his enlightened principles by his successors, among them Dr Osborne, who was Stewart's physician.

The fourth annual *Report of the Cork Lunatic Asylum* released in 1830 contains the following:

The unfortunate Captain Stewart has been

278

an inmate of the Asylum since last September and a more wretched case of insanity has seldom entered these walls, his character as an individual of the species being nearly perverted. For four months after his admission he was obliged to be, with little intermission, confined to his cell, and mostly secured to his bed, the natural impetuosity of his disposition, extorting itself in ravings and violence, in clamour and constant vociferation. Everything within his reach, even his bed clothes, was torn to pieces. His appetite was voracious, devouring all descriptions of food with avidity, muttering to himself, and as if unconscious of the act, occasionally crying in the most piteous manner not to let him be starved, but to give him anything to relieve the intolerable hunger from which he suffered. He at one time repels with rudeness those who visit him — at another, expresses obligations to them for their past kindness. On every occasion, he affirms that he is an object of human persecution, and justifies his late dreadful acts by asserting the mutinous intention of his shipmates. There are several persons who, even at this late period, affect to disbelieve the insanity of this wretched man, from the method observed by him in accomplishing those most frightful murders. But, they should know, that design and contrivance are of themselves no proof of sound mind, more particularly when connected with delusion, and unreasonable conduct . . . A competent tribunal, of intelligence commensurate with the importance of the case, has after a long and patient scrutiny, pronounced against it, and declared that the horrible acts which will be forever associated with his name were not his acts, but the acts of his distemper.

The admission of Stewart produced a strong sensation amongst the Lunatics; many entering the most absurd apprehensions for their personal safety. Those fears after a time subsided, but the aversion with which they still regard him makes it prudent that he should not be permitted to mix with them unattended by a keeper.

Now Captain Stewart was truly conforming to the behaviour expected of a madman. Scoresby describes a sketch in his possession made of Stewart by a fellow inmate:

It represents him throwing off his blanket — his sole covering — and stretching out his arms, with his uplifted countenance, towards Heaven, while he energetically and solemnly protested his innocence of the crime with which he had been charged.

In the late eighteenth century lunatics and idiots were increasingly perceived as a public nuisance, disrupting the routine at workhouses or in gaols, and there was mounting pressure to create separate, more appropriate quarters for them. Reformers gained parliamentary support for the establishment of four public Irish lunatic asylums providing a total of a thousand beds for 'pauper lunatics' (as Captain Stewart was now officially classified) to augment the totally inadequate 250 beds previously available. Captain Stewart was fortunate that Ireland was at the time leading the western world in the provision of public asylums for the destitute insane, where they would be cared for on the principles of 'moral management', in which it was hoped to effect a cure, or at least achieve some improvement by hospitalisation. Moral management was based on the idea that the patient should have a relatively normal human relationship with their doctor, and have a good environment and diet, rather than just being drugged. It was basically a humane and caring approach on an individual level, though it did rely on long-term institutional residency.

As Oliver Sacks pointed out recently (in

281

the *New York Review of Books, 2009,* Vol. *LVI,* No. 14, pp. 50–51), our attitude to mental hospitals, previously known as lunatic asylums, is based on the large and usually rather grim institutions that had evolved by the 1950s and 1960s, providing long term accommodation for the insane, who in many instances were given little or no treatment, and never expected to come out of them alive. Such long-term institutions have now largely been replaced by care in the community and sheltered housing, but their reputation as heartless penitentiaries persists.

Sacks reminds us that 'asylum' in its original usage meant refuge, protection or sanctuary, and is defined by the *Oxford English Dictionary* as 'a benevolent institution according shelter and support to some class of the afflicted, the unfortunate or destitute'. The original intention of the enlightened politicians and philanthropists who founded lunatic asylums in the nineteenth century was to provide a safe place for those judged insane by a court of law. Those sent to asylums were often profoundly relieved to be in a place that would protect them from themselves (for example, homicidal or suicidal impulses), and recognise their madness. An asylum would free them from the ridicule, aggression and abuse with which they were treated in the outside world, and give them understanding and kindness, as Sacks writes: 'Asylums offered a life with its own special protections and limitations, a simplified and narrowed life perhaps, but within this protective structure, the freedom to be as mad as one liked and, for some patients at least, to live through their psychoses and emerge from their depths as saner and stabler people.' Captain Stewart appears to be very grateful for the protective environment offered to him by the Cork asylum.

Under the asylum's regime, Stewart was slowly recovering, writes Scoresby: 'His previous excitement and violence had changed, by ordinary reaction, into anxiety and depression. And still, on some points, he continued decidedly insane.' Nevertheless, on hearing that Scoresby was in Cork, Stewart expressed a desire to see him. Scoresby found Stewart's mind 'greatly harassed, with similar fears of personal injury being designed against him, as had possessed him when he committed the dreadful act for which he was incarcerated'. When Scoresby arrived, Stewart thought God had sent him to console him in his affliction. The events on the *Mary Russell* were haunting him. He told Scoresby that he knew he had been wrong to attack

John Howes in the hold, because the thought had gone through his mind that he might possibly be innocent. For this, he feared God was angry with him, and that he would suffer. His conscience was also paining him for another circumstance: 'When poor Raynes lay bound in the cabin, he mentioned the name of God; but thinking it was hypocrisy, I then reproached him, saying 'The devil is your God'.' Scoresby continues, in a key passage:

He was further distressed by the belief that an opinion had gone abroad that he was a vile *murderer* — a report so unjust to himself, and so injurious to his family. I told him that I had taken notes respecting his case, which, if published, might serve to remove such an impression where it unhappily prevailed.

So Scoresby now had a rationale for writing his narrative, *The Mary Russell*, and the approval of its chief protagonist.

At their parting, the Reverend Scoresby offered some soothing words of comfort and indeed provided direction for the agitated captain, in one of the nautical metaphors for which his sermons were famous. He told him 'to strive to fix the anchor of his soul on the consolations of the Gospel, rather than drift

284

away in the current of despair'. At which point, Stewart grapsed Scoresby's hand and his eyes filled with tears as he said 'May God bless you. You have done me much good: I know that God has sent you to me in mercy; you have spoken by the Spirit of God, for I feel it in my heart.'

The two sea captains last met on 16 November 1831 in the Cork Lunatic Asylum. Stewart was calm and comparatively rational, and had been for some months. He was busy rigging and finishing off a large model of a ship, 5 or 6 feet long: 'It was in good taste, of correct proportions, and of really clever workmanship,' wrote Scoresby. Stewart hoped to sell it in order to obtain some help for his 'almost starving family'. This initiative had been suggested by Dr Osborne, and approved by the governor, in line with the asylum's policy, and turned into a successful venture. (Dr Brendan Kelly comments that the obsessive attention to detail involved in the building of fully rigged model ships is entirely consistent with the diagnosis of bipolar disease rather than schizophrenia.)

Stewart spent a great deal of his time choosing beef and mutton bones left after the patients' meals for use in his model ship building. Although the asylum encouraged his enterprise, he was not allowed to use a knife, but he used a very hard bone to carve the decorations, and he spent many hours polishing them until they shone. He carefully built and rigged a small model ship, measuring 21 inches from bow to stern, and 251/2 inches tall, and presented it to Dr Osborne. In 1833 Stewart wrote to Scoresby:

You will be pleased to hear that my little mechanical works, which you directed me to pursue, have added many pounds to the support of my family, for which I am truly grateful to the Doctor and the Governor, who have at all times encouraged me and greatly assisted me.

We learn from these letters that Captain Stewart is comfortable in the asylum under Dr Osborne's care. He reports that the diet is good, and that he enjoys great privileges.

Dr Hallaran, in his book on the causes and cures of insanity, identifies four main causes of insanity: hereditary disease; abuse of spirituous liquors; war, foreign and domestic; and religious dread. Religious dread or mania had been identified by previous authors on the subject, both English and German. Hallaran makes this interesting observation about the situation in Ireland:

In our public asylum, which is inhabited by persons of the Roman Catholic persuasion, in the proportion of ten to one of the established Church, no instance, within my recollection, has occurred of mental derangement in the former, from religious enthusiasm.

Of those who succumb to religious enthusiasm, he writes 'They are unfortunately the most obstinate, and the least disposed to submit to the necessary modes of treatment, and are peculiarly liable to returns of the complaint.'

From 1832 to 1834 Stewart and Scoresby regularly exchanged letters, mostly about religious matters. The chapter 'Letters from Captain Stewart' in William Scoresby's narrative, would seem to suggest that Stewart had become obsessed with religion to the point of mania. Consider the beginning of the letter dated 3 September 1834:

My dear Revered friend — It behoves us all to attend to what our blessed Saviour says to all — *Watch!* For it is certain we know not the hour of his coming. What a blessing it is when the Lord takes us in hand to chasten us for our profit! Though human nature thinks no chastening for the present joyous, but grievous; nevertheless afterward it yieldeth the peaceable fruits of righteousness to them that are exercised thereby.

The letter continues for three more pages in similar vein. But rather than seeing it as evidence of religious mania, Scoresby sees it as 'in no small measure accordant with the scripturally described characteristics of one sincerely repentant.' Was Stewart writing in this way to gain the approval of his Reverend friend? Or did his mind run continually along these lines in all his waking hours?

In summing up his conclusions, there are two areas in which Scoresby, very gently, once again finds fault with Captain Stewart's behaviour on the fateful journey. The first is with his use of 'ardent spirits' [strong drink], which he should have avoided, coming from a hot climate, and knowing that he had a tendency to overexcitement. The other is described in the next chapter, 'On the Nature and Discrimination of Providential Guidance', and is rather more complicated. In summary, Scoresby's argument states that the most serious mistake Captain Stewart made was to interpret certain events on his voyage as Providence giving him signs. He also referred to Providence as 'the hand of God' and 'the finger of God' pointing things out to him. The most crucial occasion was when the second boat failed to make contact with the *Mary Russell*, which Stewart interpreted as meaning that God was telling him that his men were damned, and therefore he was obliged to kill them. But in fact, says Scoresby, Providence was not giving him signs; Stewart was confusing the manifestations of Providence with superstition. That which is called 'fate' by heathens and sceptics, 'we, by the revelation of God, do certainly know to belong to a wise and particular Providence'. Scoresby quotes Ecclesiastes: there is 'a time to be born, and a time to die'. Elsewhere he declares that these times are not determined by fate or chance, but by the Lord, 'For the Lord ruleth in the earth, and 'our times are in his hand.' How could God permit the terrible calamity that we have been considering, he asks. And he answers:

Hence, inscrutable as the ways of Providence in some dispensations necessarily are, yet by the guidance of Revelation and the analogies of Faith, we may in many cases discern, a purpose of goodness, and an act of mercy. Those among the helpless sufferers in the catastrophe before us ... experienced in the murderous act, a release from a life of toil and suffering, to be advanced to speedy felicity and glory.

In other words, the victims of Captain Stewart's mania did not die prematurely in an arbitrary way: they were hastened out of this life of toil to be advanced to heavenly glory. According to the religious thinking of the time, they were, in their way, fortunate.

★   ★   ★

In March 1840, Captain Stewart had a visit from Mr and Mrs Hall, whose descriptions of their journey around Ireland have already been quoted. The unabridged edition of their book contains an account of their visit to Captain Stewart in the Cork Lunatic Asylum. Having briefly described the events on the *Mary Russell*, they describe the murderer (to whom they refer as 'Steward'):

Steward is a small and slight man, now apparently under fifty years of age [in fact he was 65]. He was dressed in sailor's garb, remarkably neat and clean. He conversed with us freely upon ordinary topics and referred to the time he was in jail, without however alluding to the crime for which he had been imprisoned. There is, to our minds no expression in his countenance that indicates insanity; and certainly, it is by no means characteristic of ferocity. His visage is thin, long, and pallid; his mouth narrow, close and inflexible; his eyes small, grey, restless and very acute — more like the eyes of a rat than a human being. We understand that he frequently speaks of the murders he committed, and always as necessary for the preservation of his own life from the plots of his mutinous crew. We confess that his absence was a relief; for it was impossible to avoid recalling to remembrance the appalling deed which had made so many parents childless; or to look upon this wretched man without feeling akin to loathing.

Their account is spine-chilling — 'eyes more like a rat than a human being' — but it is at least honest. It recalls Reverend Scoresby's awestruck reaction back in 1828, when he found himself shaking the hand that had killed seven men only two weeks before.

Dr Osborne died in 1845. Stewart remained in the Cork Asylum until 1851 and the opening in Dublin of the Dundrum Asylum for the Criminally Insane with accommodation for 120 inmates. Here he passed away on 21 August 1873 at the age of 98, suffering from senile decay, according to an article in the *Journal of the Cork Historical and Archaeological Society* (1905), 'Souvenir of the *Mary Russell* Tragedy'. It is believed that he is buried in St Nahi's Cemetery, Churchtown Parish, Dundrum, to the left of the entrance gates in a communal plot, originally a mass Famine grave, later used by the asylum. There is no record of what became of his wife, Betsy.

24

Mutiny and Piracy

Because the issue of mutiny is central to the story of the massacre on the *Mary Russell*, it is important to understand what mutiny meant to seafarers at the time. While Captain Stewart's suspicions of a mutinous plot on board the *Mary Russell* were an unfounded product of his deteriorating mental state, fear of mutiny was widespread among naval captains of the time, as was fear of attacks by pirates. Both mutiny and piracy were serious crimes, punishable by death. Suppression of piracy and mutiny was essential in order to maintain naval discipline. Pirates were not always attackers from another boat. Once a sailor had disobeyed orders and become a mutineer, he was also considered a pirate, and referred to as such.

Mutiny, in its simplest definition, is a conspiracy among a group of individuals to oppose or overthrow the authority above them. It can consist of something as simple as refusing to obey an order, or as dramatic as overpowering and killing the person in authority. Obedience to orders is at the heart of naval discipline. In time of war, obedience to orders was the glue that bound a mixed gang of raw recruits, forcibly impressed men and volunteers, into a loyal ship's company. The captain's word was law, and nobody on board dared to question or contradict it. To do so, was considered mutiny. Anyone who disobeyed or disrespected the captain or any superior officer had to be dealt with sternly, hence the death penalty for the crime of mutiny. Naval officers were always outnumbered by the men below decks, and a mob of men that got out of hand could easily overpower and kill the commanding officer. Suppression of mutinous tendencies also lay behind the reputation of some captains in both the Royal Navy and the merchant navy for cruelty. Naval discipline was violent, with flogging — being publicly whipped on the bare back while tied to the mast — the penalty for many offences from insubordination to blasphemy. From this distance the behaviour of many captains smacks of sadism, but such extreme and cruel measures were sanctioned in the cause of maintaining shipboard discipline. A captain on board a ship of the line needed to keep as many as 800 men in order with only a handful of officers, and sometimes a small number of armed marines.

In the Royal Navy, where many captains of

the merchant marine had learnt their trade, the rules were spelt out by a code of behaviour known as the Articles of War. These were laid down at the foundation of the Royal Navy following the Restoration of King Charles II in 1661, and were written by Samuel Pepys and Admiral Sir William Penn (whose son was the founder of Pennsylvania). On warships of the Royal Navy they had the status of Holy Writ, and were often read in full on Sunday in place of a church service. Mutiny is covered under Article XIX: 'If any person in or belonging to the Fleet shall make or endeavour to make any mutinous Assembly upon any Pretence whatsoever, every Person offending herein, and being convicted thereof by the Sentence of the Court-martial, shall suffer Death.'

Mention mutiny nowadays, and the first thing that comes into most people's minds is the mutiny on the *Bounty*. Even though this happened in the generation before the voyage of the *Mary Russell*, Captain Bligh's memoir of the mutiny was published in 1790, and the events and characters of the voyage had become part of popular culture by 1828. By the time the survivors of the *Bounty* were tried for mutiny in 1792, Captain Stewart was seventeen, and whether he was already stationed at the naval base at Chatham in

Kent, or still living with his parents in Cove, the mutiny on the *Bounty* would have been a compelling topic of conversation.

The three men found guilty, John Millward, Thomas Burkett and Thomas Ellison, were sentenced to be publicly hanged from the yardarm of HMS *Brunswick* in Portsmouth Harbour on Monday 29 October 1792. A huge crowd had gathered along the shore and aboard other boats to witness the execution, as described by Caroline Alexander in her excellent account of the true story of the mutiny, *Bounty* (London, 2003):

Bags were placed over the heads of each man, and now nooses were placed around their necks. At 11.26, according to Curtis's log, the gun was fired for execution, and the crew assigned to each prisoner's rope pulled hard away, swinging the bodies up to the yardarm. 'Thomas Burkett was Run up to the Starboard fore Yard Arm, Milward and Ellison to the Larboard, and There Hung Agreeable to their sentence,' Curtis logged.

The bodies of the executed men were left hanging from the yards for two hours in heavy rain before being cut down and ferried across the water to the naval hospital for burial.

HMS *Bounty* had sailed for Tahiti in August 1787 under the patronage of Sir Joseph Banks (who was also a patron of William Scoresby, and most of the important scientists of the time). Bligh had proved his ability as navigator and cartographer on Captain Cook's third and final voyage, on which he had served as master of the *Resolution*. The *Bounty's* mission was to land on Tahiti, secure as many healthy breadfruit as possible, and deliver them to the West Indies where it was hoped they would thrive and provide cheap but nutritious food for the plantation slaves. The 30,000-mile round trip was expected to take about two years. If Bligh had been promoted to Post-Captain prior to the voyage, he would have been allocated a junior commissioned officer to reinforce his authority, but as it was he had to sail with only warrant officers and midshipmen. Neither was he entitled to have any armed marines aboard to back him up, even though he had requested some. In spite of having a crew of thirty, the ship was considered undermanned, and in many cases Bligh did not have much say in who was enlisted. Tensions with two of the warrant officers, the carpenter and the sailing master, arose on the long outward journey. On reaching the island, famed for its friendly natives and sexually uninhibited women, three of the seamen tried to desert and were flogged. A relatively minor dispute led to the Master Mate, Fletcher Christian, leading a band of seamen and taking over the boat. Captain Bligh and eighteen of the crew were set adrift in the ship's 23-foot launch with few provisions, and navigated 3,618 miles (6,701 km) to Timor on the coast of Java, arriving more dead than alive forty-eight days later. Bligh returned to England on 14 March 1790, and having returned without his ship was subject to a court martial. This was held on 22 October: he was acquitted and promoted to captain in December. Also in 1790 he published his account of the mutiny, *A Narrative of the Mutiny on Board His Majesty's Ship Bounty; and the Subsequent Voyage of Part of the Crew, in the Ship's Boat, from Tofoa, one of the Friendly Islands, to Timor, a Dutch Settlement in the East Indies.*

In August 1791, Bligh set off on his second breadfruit expedition which this time included a party of marines. While he was away, the *Pandora*, which had been dispatched to the South Seas to apprehend the mutineers, returned to Britain, and the mutineers were tried in his absence. Their testimony emphasised his quick temper and sharp tongue, tarnishing his reputation. Bligh has gone down in folklore as the epitome of the cruel captain, while the leader of the mutineers, Fletcher Christian, has been immortalised as the typical romantic hero, with his open shirt, his long hair flying free, defying the power of the establishment and opting for a life of sensual pleasure among the beautiful South Sea Islanders.

The story of the *Bounty* continued to unfold over the years, as the relatives of the mutineers sought to clear their names, and in the process blackening Bligh's. In 1794 Fletcher Christian's lawyer brother, Edward, published a transcript of the mutineer's trial, and Bligh replied by publishing a pamphlet refuting its contents. In 1795 a short reply to this was published by Edward Christian. Meanwhile there were rumours that Fletcher Christian, who had been a schoolmate of the poet Wordsworth at Cockermouth Free School in Cumberland, had been seen in his native home. In 1810 an American seal-hunting vessel, the *Topaz* under Captain Folger, landed at Pitcairn Island and met the sole surviving mutineer, Alexander Smith, aka John Adams. He confirmed that Fletcher had been killed on Pitcairn, shot in the back while digging yams, in the course of a dispute between the mutineers and the Tahitians. (Bligh's subsequent career led him to Dublin in 1800, where he used his skills as a cartographer to survey Dublin Bay, and designed the North and South Bull Walls to clear a sandbar at the mouth of the bay. This led to the formation of the Bull Island.) He died and was buried in London in 1817.

Caroline Alexander traces the way that the story caught the imagination of a generation of poets, from the minor and now forgotten Mary Russell Mitford (*Christina, the Maid of the South Seas*, 1811) to the famous Lord Byron. In 1821 a well-travelled Tahitian known as Jenny, the widow of a mutineer, published her version of the story, and this was followed in 1831 by the first comprehensive account of the various dramas that make up the story of the mutiny on the *Bounty: The Eventful History of the Mutiny and Piratical Seizure of H.M.S. Bounty; its Causes and Consequences*. Published anonymously, this turned out to be written by Sir John Barrow, second secretary at the Admiralty, and a family friend of one of the survivors of the *Bounty*. It was the first in a long stream of book-length works about the incident, which is being added to even now, in both fact and fiction, over 200 years after the event.

While there is no direct relation between the mutiny off Tahiti on the Royal Navy's ship

Bounty and the imagined mutiny off the coast of Ireland aboard the humble merchant ship, the *Mary Russell*, with its crew of twelve and its humdrum cargo of sugar and skins, the *Bounty* is nevertheless important to Captain Stewart's story. It is quite possibly the root cause of some of his deepest fears, and the reason why he had a roster of men sleeping outside his cabin, and why he eventually ceased to take any rest at all. Captain Bligh always slept with his cabin door open, and was asleep during the night of 28 April 1789 when Fletcher Christian burst into his cabin with a gang of armed men, and struck him on the chest with the flat of a cutlass. This is how Captain Bligh describes the incident in his *Narrative*:

Just before sun-rising, Mr. Christian, with the master-at-arms, gunner's mate, and Thomas Burket, seaman, came into my cabin while I was asleep and, seizing me, tied my hands with a cord behind my back, and threatened me with instant death, if I spoke or made the least noise: I, however, called so loud as to alarm everyone; but they had already secured the officers who were not of their party, by placing centinels [sic] at their doors. There were three men at my cabin door, besides the four within;

Christian had only a cutlass in his hand, the others had muskets and bayonets. I was hauled out of bed, and forced on deck in my shirt, suffering great pain from the tightness with which they had tied my hands. I demanded the reason of such violence, but received no other answer than threats of instant death, if I did not hold my tongue . . . The boatswain was now ordered to hoist the launch out, with a threat if he did not do it instantly, to take care of himself. The boat being hoisted out, Mr. Hayward and Mr. Hallet, midshipmen, and Mr Samuel were ordered into it; upon which I demanded the cause of such an order, and endeavoured to persuade some one to a sense of duty; but it was to no effect: 'Hold your tongue, sir, or you are dead this instant,' was constantly repeated to me.

The image was immortalised by the poet Byron in *The Island* (1823), where he refers to Bligh as 'the gallant Chief'.

The gallant Chief within his cabin slept,
Secure in those by whom the watch was
    kept:
His dreams were of Old England's wel-
    come shore,
Of toils rewarded, and of dangers o'er;

Byron's poem assumes that the lusty young mutineers have resolved to take charge of the ship in order to return to the women on their paradise-like South Sea island. The poet attempts to warn the captain of what is to come:

> Awake, bold Bligh! The foe is at the
>   gate!
> Awake! Awake! Alas it is too late!
> Fiercely beside thy cot the mutineer
> Stands, and proclaims the reign of rage
>   and fear.
> Thy limbs are bound, the bayonet at
>   thy breast;
> The hands, which trembled at thy voice,
>   arrest;

Stewart's persistent fear of being murdered in his bed echoes Bligh's experience, and also that of many other mariners who had been subject to attacks by mutineers or pirates.

The *Annual Register* for 1828, which devotes six pages to an account of the 'Singular Murder' on board the *Mary Russell*, contains a smaller half-page item earlier in the same year under the heading *Mutiny and Murder*. This recounts an incident on board the *Thetis*, a 250-ton brig sailing from Sierra Leone to Cork that again closely echoes the fears that bedevilled Captain Stewart. The *Thetis*, under Captain John Bailie, left Bristol for Sierra Leone on 7 February 1828 and arrived on 8 April. Eight of the twelve crew were left in Africa owing to sickness, and were replaced by four Portuguese. So the ship was being sailed by a small crew consisting of four Portuguese speakers and four Englishmen. On 2 June the *Thetis* left Sierra Leone for Cork. On the night of 31 July the captain retired to bed at ten o'clock, as was his usual custom. At half-past ten he was awoken by three loud knocks on the deck. He jumped out of bed, and was about to go up on deck when he found one of the Portuguese men, Francis Domingo, at his door with an axe and a knife in his hands. When Captain Bailie approached him, Domingo aimed the axe at his head, which Bailie managed to dodge, but Domingo plunged his knife into the captain's arm. The captain wrested the axe out of Domingo's hand, and retreated quickly back into his cabin. As he did so, one of the English sailors, Francis Smith, came running down from the deck, with his throat cut open and his right shoulder wounded by a knife. Three of the English crew were now below, while the fourth, Matthews, remained on the deck, which was now held by the Portuguese mutineers. The mutineers fastened the companionway shut, trapping the English crew and captain in the cabin. Captain Bailie wrote a letter describing the incident, which he sealed in a bottle and threw overboard through the cabin window. At three in the morning, the mutineers struck a light on deck, lowered the boats from the vessel, and filled them with every portable article on board. They then set fire to the vessel, and stayed by her in the boats until three in the afternoon. At this point Captain Bailie saw the boats go astern, and he and his two comrades managed to release themselves and get up on deck. They found the ship in flames from the fore part to the mainmast, and saw a large quantity of blood, which they concluded must have been Matthews'. Unable to extinguish the fire, they built a small raft, and 'committed themselves to Providence'. The sea was calm, and they sat on the raft, watching as the fire extended to every part of the ship, eventually sinking her. Captain Bailie steered the raft northwards for three days and nights, and on the fourth day, he and his companions having subsisted on a small amount of bread, with no fresh water, were picked up by a vessel bound for Liverpool.

The parallels with Captain Stewart's fears

are even clearer here: the non-English speaking crew conspiring together against their captain and his English-speaking compatriots.

Captain Stewart could not have heard this particular story, as the mutiny took place in late July, by which time he was already in Cork County Gaol. The point of the anecdote is that incidents of piracy were still occurring on the high seas, even in these more peaceful times. During the five weeks that the *Mary Russell* spent in Bridgetown, the busy harbour of Barbados, Stewart and his crew would have met many fellow mariners with spicy tales like this one to tell, some of which could well have helped to build fears in the anxious captain's potentially unstable mind.

In particular, at this era, the sea between the coast of West Africa and the Cape Verde Islands, near the route that the *Mary Russell* would have followed, was a rich hunting ground for pirates in the aftermath of the abolition of slavery. They were still active in 1830, according to this item in the Ship News of the *Cork Constitution* on 2 June 1830:

The East India Company's schooner, *St. Helena*, Harrison, has been taken and plundered by pirates who killed the Captain, the Chief Officer Dr Waddle, and

306

then scuttled and abandoned her. The carpenter, however, and five men succeeded in bringing her into Sierra Leone.

Piracy has been with us as long as ships have been on the sea. A pirate is defined as a robber who preys on other ships, with the aim of stealing their cargo or capturing the ship itself for their own purposes. In times of war, pirates operated from privateers, which were privately owned boats, licensed by their governments with letters of marque, to harass the enemy's shipping, and keep the profits. Letters of marque were finally banned in 1856 by the Declaration of Paris.

The Golden Age of piracy, which has inspired so many stories and films, most recently the *Pirates of the Caribbean* series, ran roughly from 1620 to 1750. Those involved were known as buccaneers, and operated from bases in the West Indies, initially attacking Spanish shipping in the Caribbean. The most sought-after prize would be a Spanish galleon returning from the newly conquered South American colonies laden with Aztec and Inca gold.

The growth of the slave trade, in which slaves were transported from the West African coast to the sugar plantations of the West Indies and to the mainland American coast of the Gulf of Mexico, gave further scope to the buccaneer. Given the harsh conditions on board ships of both the Royal Navy and the merchant marine, piracy was an attractive alternative, offering a better life often with a fair and democratic organisation guaranteeing every sailor a share of the prize money, and offering a lottery-like chance of becoming rich and settling down on land to start a new life.

Two things put an end to the so-called Golden Age of piracy: first the establishment of colonial settlements belonging to France, Britain, the Netherlands, Portugal and Spain in the Caribbean, which led to the increasing presence of warships in the area, and secondly the outlawing of the slave trade.

The slave trade operated on a triangular pattern, as generations of schoolchildren used to be taught. Ships from Britain and continental Europe travelled to the Slave Coast (the Bight of Benin in West Africa) with a cargo of guns, fabrics, hardware and glittering (but worthless) jewellery, and supplies of rum and brandy.

Gold and ivory had first attracted European traders to this shore, but the establishment of sugar plantations in the West Indies created a market for slaves. Men, women and children from the African interior were offered to the foreign ships by coastal Africans. Laden to the gunwales with slaves, the ships then sailed the Middle Passage, transatlantic to the West Indies where the slaves were sold at auction to the highest bidder. The boats were then loaded up with sugar, spices and other expensive exotica, and sailed back to Europe. Within the United Kingdom, London, Bristol and Liverpool were the principal slave ports. Both Bristol and Liverpool were said to be 'built on the slave trade', as most of their public buildings date from the economic expansion of those years.

The campaign against the slave trade began in 1787, but it was not until March 1807 that both Britain and America passed acts to outlaw the slave trade from January 1808. But while the buying and selling of slaves was outlawed, slavery itself was not abolished in British territories until 1833. A civil war was fought over its abolition in the US, which finally took place in 1865; in Brazil slavery continued to be legal until 1871.

So with the world divided on the issue of slavery, it was not surprising that the slave trade continued after it had been officially abolished by the Britain and the US. The British and American navies took it on themselves to intercept slave traders that were continuing to traffic in enslaved human beings, and release their cargo of slaves in Freetown, Sierra Leone.

One such incident is recorded in his personal log by a young Corkman, Richard Roberts, who was to become famous in 1838 as the first man to captain a scheduled passenger steamer, the *Sirius*, across the Atlantic. On 15 June 1828, while the *Mary Russell* was on her homeward passage from Barbados, Dick Roberts was a young midshipman in the Royal Navy aboard HMS *Medina*, when it arrived in Lisbon en route for Gambia and Sierra Leone. Later in the same trip, Roberts had his first taste of action on 3 October 1828 when the *Medina* chased a Brazilian schooner, *Penha de Franca*, overtook her, fired at her, boarded her and accepted her surrender. The Brazilian boat had been carrying 184 slaves. Roberts was put in charge of the prize schooner, and sailed her to Freetown, Sierra Leone, where the slaves were released. (A full account of this incident can be found in Daphne Pochin Mould's biography, *Captain Roberts of the Sirius*, Cork, 1988)

While the *Mary Russell*'s course lay to the north of this coast, both captain and crew would have been aware that these were unsettled times, and out in the open sea, many miles from land, and with no means of

310

communication, one had to be wary of all other shipping. Incidents of piracy had decreased since their height in the mid-eighteenth century, but Captain Stewart was well aware that there were still desperate, lawless types afloat. His genuine fear of attack by pirates heightened his imaginary fear of a mutiny on board.

As to the question of why the crew of the *Mary Russell* did not resist their captain by restraining him while at sea and taking control of the boat, the answer is very simple: that would have been mutiny, a capital offence, and the burden would have been on the men to prove that their captain was mad. And if they could not do so, they would automatically face the death penalty. It was not a risk any of them, not even the redoubtable Howes, was prepared to take. There was simply no provision for dealing with a captain who had gone mad at sea, and his unfortunate crew and passengers suffered the consequences.

Postscript

This book is based on a thesis written by Kathy Bunney at Coláiste Stiofín Naofa on an Access to Social Studies Course in 2008–9. Kathy is an adult returning to education in mid-life, and the mother of six boys.

She discovered the story of Captain Stewart and the murders aboard the *Mary Russell* while working on a local history project. This involved reading the oral material gathered in 1937 by a local school from older members of the community, and written down by its students, for the Folklore Commission. Kathy chose the Star of the Sea National School in the parish of Marmullane in Passage, and it was among the school's folklore collection (available on microfilm at Cork County Library) that she first read a version of Captain Stewart's story.

Her research thereafter consisted of a unique combination of intuition, old-fashioned foot-slogging, and intensive internet use. A chance encounter led her to the house in Cobh, which is said to have belonged to Captain Stewart. It is believed locally that his sons and grandsons went on to become sea captains, and moved to Liverpool. But there was little factual information to be had on Captain Stewart in Cobh. A major event was the discovery, after an hour and a half of searching among the overgrown graves in Kilmurray Graveyard, high above the town of Passage West, of Timothy Connell's tombstone, with its inscription describing the manner of his death.

The newspaper archive in the Cork County Library with their contemporary reports of the inquest and trial provided a wealth of factual material. Another major breakthrough came with the discovery on googlebooks of William Scoresby's *Memorials of the Sea* (1835) with its meticulously detailed, 167-page account of the voyage, inquest and trial, simply entitled *The Mary Russell*.

This information allowed Kathy to identify the errors in the few twentieth-century retellings of the story. These began with an article in the *Journal of the Cork Historical and Archaeological Society* in 1905, which contains a picture of the bone boat made by Captain Stewart for Dr Osborne (this was on show in the Cork Exhibition of 1902–3 and has not been seen since). Stewart's name is variously Seymour and Steward in the crude retellings which emerged intermittently throughout the twentieth century, as shock-horror 'fillers' in regatta programmes and local newspapers. The resulting 141-page thesis had 414 footnotes, and was illustrated with images taken on digital camera of relevant buildings and documents, and hand-drawn illustrations by Enya MacMahon. Kathy's course director, Shane Lehane, was so impressed that he showed the thesis to The Collins Press, in the belief that there was a book in it. I was asked to rewrite and expand it. When Kathy handed it over to me it was accompanied by three heavy ring-binders of additional material.

Most of the writing is mine, but Kathy Bunney and I are very much co-authors of this project, with her input being the animating force. There is more to a book like this than just writing. Throughout the time I worked on it, Kathy was available to chase up leads and ferret out facts, in spite of the demands of her busy life. We have had many lively discussions about Captain Stewart and his crew. One of the biggest breakthroughs was Kathy's discovery of Captain Stewart's date of birth, and the record of his marriage. Without Kathy this book would not have existed. It is the result of her commitment to learning about ourselves from local history by listening to the stories the older generations have to tell.

But it also highlights how quickly even the

most extraordinary events disappear from memory. If it had not been for the 1937 Folklore Collection, we might never have discovered the story of the ship of seven murders. Of the seven men who died, we have found only one grave. There were no death notices at the time, and funerals were not reported. We do not know what happened to the three apprentices and the survivors Smith and Howes. The grave of the child Thomas Hammond and his parents was located with the help of records from a FÁS scheme that identified unmarked graves in Cobh. T. Hammond was buried in the grave in 1829, Mary (his mother) in 1849 and James (his father) in 1869. Nothing more is heard of Betsy Stewart after 1828, and there is no trace of any descendants of the Stewart family, nor of the descendants of any of the men on board the ship. Strangest of all, we have not been able to discover the identity of the person who is still looking after Timothy Connell's grave in Passage.

Alannah Hopkin